Unit C

Pass the Word

Using Energy and Technology

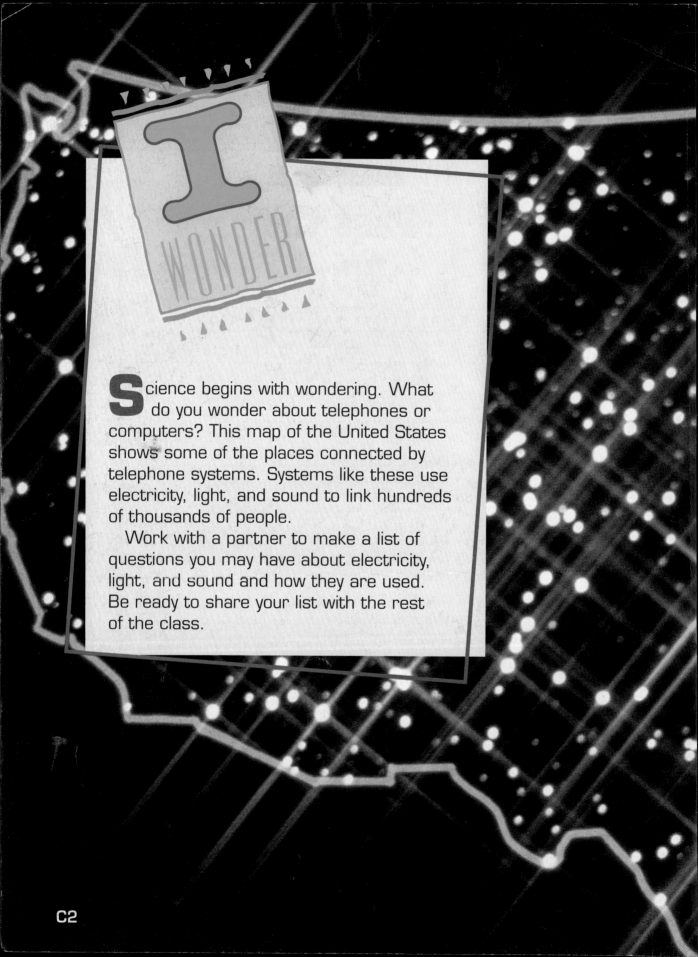

I WONDER

Science begins with wondering. What do you wonder about telephones or computers? This map of the United States shows some of the places connected by telephone systems. Systems like these use electricity, light, and sound to link hundreds of thousands of people.

Work with a partner to make a list of questions you may have about electricity, light, and sound and how they are used. Be ready to share your list with the rest of the class.

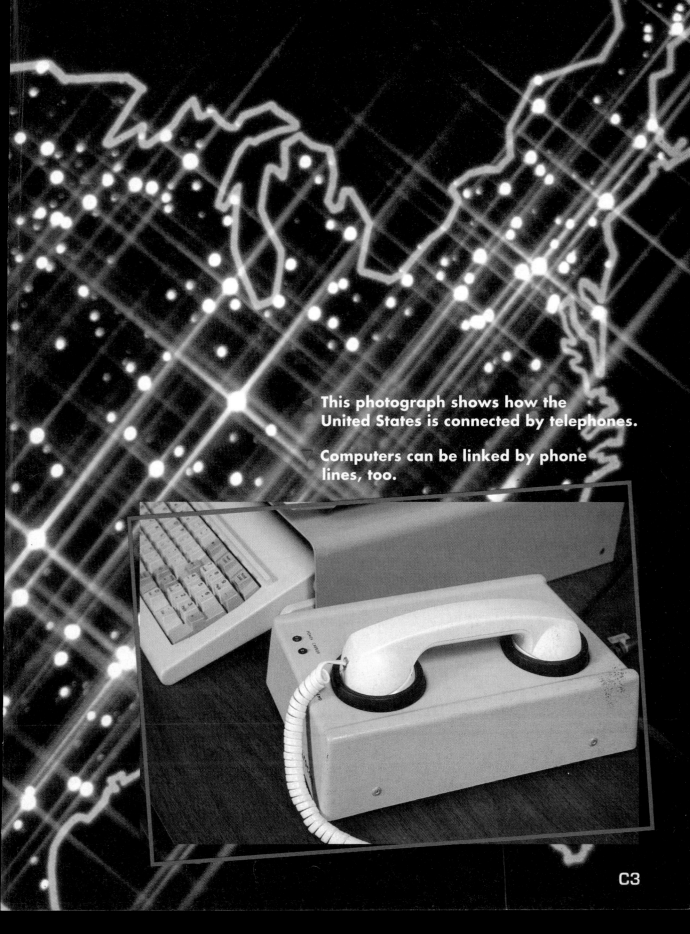

This photograph shows how the
United States is connected by telephones.

Computers can be linked by phone
lines, too.

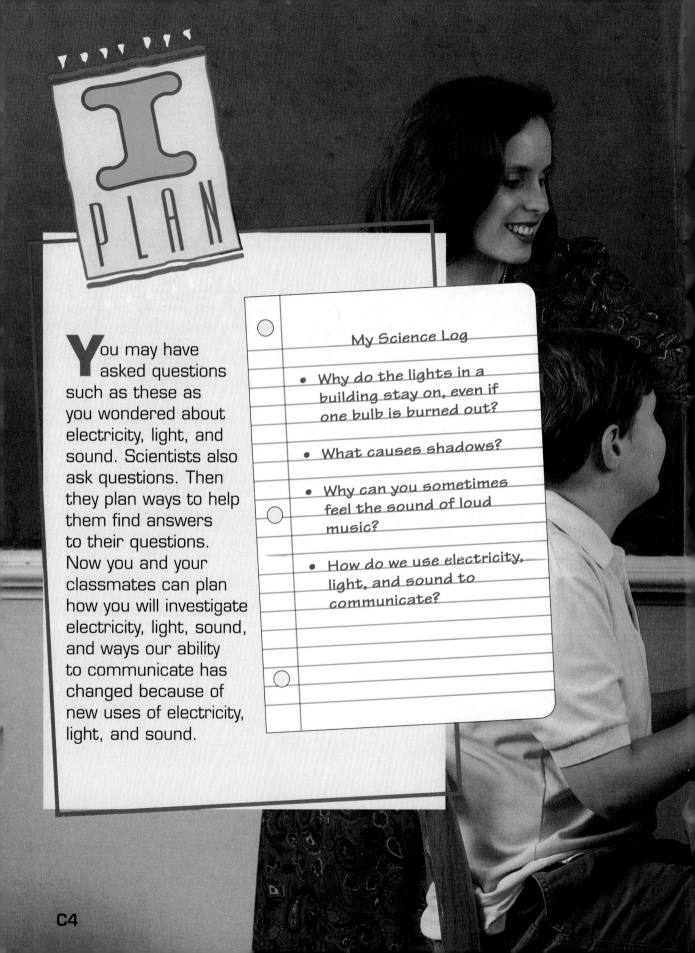

I PLAN

You may have asked questions such as these as you wondered about electricity, light, and sound. Scientists also ask questions. Then they plan ways to help them find answers to their questions. Now you and your classmates can plan how you will investigate electricity, light, sound, and ways our ability to communicate has changed because of new uses of electricity, light, and sound.

My Science Log

- Why do the lights in a building stay on, even if one bulb is burned out?

- What causes shadows?

- Why can you sometimes feel the sound of loud music?

- How do we use electricity, light, and sound to communicate?

Plans

With Your Class

Plan how your class will use the activities and readings from the **I Investigate** part of this unit.

On Your Own

There are many ways to learn about electricity, light, and sound. As you study this unit, you will read and do activities during class time. Following are some things you can do to explore electricity, light, and sound by yourself or with some classmates. Some explorations may take longer to do than others. Look over the suggestions and choose…

- **Projects to Do**
- **Places to Visit**
- **Books to Read**

PROJECTS TO DO

SCIENCE FAIR PROJECT

Investigate shadows. Observe them at different times of the day. Observe shadows made by different objects. Find out why some shadows are darker than others. Take photographs of interesting shadows. Then write captions for the photographs, explaining what you have found out about shadows. Have people guess what made the shadows in your photographs.

TIME LINES

Work with a partner. Choose one invention, such as the telephone, the camera, or the computer. Read about how this invention was developed and how it has been changed over the years. Use information from your reading to make an illustrated time line showing the development of the invention. You may also want to extend your time line into the future and predict what future improvements will be.

BROADCAST STATION

Set up a broadcasting station in your classroom. Use what you learn about sound, light, and electricity to develop a code and a method for communicating with others.

PLACES TO VISIT

NEWSROOM

Go to a local newspaper office or television station. Observe different kinds of communication equipment reporters use to find and report the news. Watch someone working on a computer to write a story or design a page. Take notes about the things you see. Then write several paragraphs comparing what the newsroom is like today with what it might have been like before the telephone, computer, and fax machine were invented.

ELECTRONICS STORE

Is there an electronics store or a telephone store in your neighborhood? With an adult, spend some time studying the electronic equipment for sale there. If the store has a videophone, observe how it works. Draw a picture of something you see there that is new to you. Write a few sentences telling what makes the invention unique.

MUSEUM

Many science and other museums have exhibits about electricity, magnets, sound, light, and electronics used for communication. Visit a nearby museum or science center where you can see exhibits of the inventions of the twentieth century.

BOOKS TO READ

In the Middle of the Night

by Kathy Henderson (Macmillan, 1992). Many people work at night while you sleep. People use light and electricity to travel, clean, cook, send mail, and do many other jobs at night that make your days better. Watching these people and listening to the sounds of the night, shows that night isn't a restful time for everyone. After a busy night, you find clean streets, fresh food, and mail in the mailboxes. In this book, you will read about the people who work at night and how light, sound, and electricity help them do their jobs.

IN THE MIDDLE OF THE NIGHT

Kathy Henderson ◆ Jennifer Eachus

Mom Can't See Me

by Sally Hobart Alexander (Macmillan, 1990). Can you imagine a world without light? How would you find things? In this book, you'll read about Leslie's mother, Mrs. Alexander. She lives in a world without light, yet she cooks, takes dancing lessons, and writes stories. Find out how she uses senses other than sight to do these things and many others.

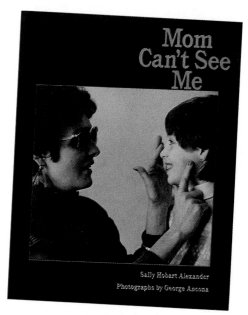

Mom Can't See Me

Sally Hobart Alexander
Photographs by George Ancona

More Books to Read

The Little Pigs' Puppet Book

by N. Cameron Watson (Little, Brown, 1990). On a rainy day, the three pig brothers decide to put on a puppet show. After you read this book, you will be able to put on a puppet show, too. You will learn about the stage, lighting, special effects, and even how to make refreshments for the audience.

Samuel Todd's Book of Great Inventions

by E. L. Konigsburg (Atheneum, 1991), Outstanding Science Trade Book. Inventions make our lives easier and better in many ways. In this book, you will find out that Samuel Todd thinks the greatest invention is the box—or maybe the mirror, the backpack, or French fries.

Here Comes the Mail

by Gloria Skurzynski (Bradbury, 1992). This book takes you on a visit to the post office to see what happens to the letters you mail. With the help of machines, postal workers sort the mail, scan it, and put it on a truck. Post office employees work night and day to deliver the mail.

The Science Book of Electricity

by Neil Ardley (Harcourt Brace, 1991). There are two kinds of electricity—static electricity and current electricity. This book shows you how to do experiments that will help you discover something about both kinds of electricity.

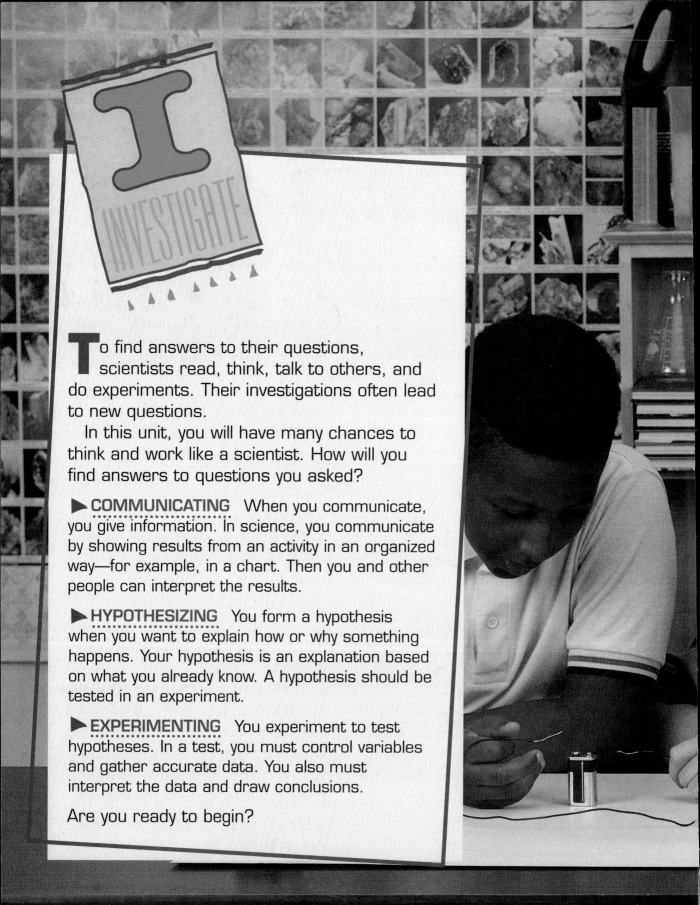

INVESTIGATE

To find answers to their questions, scientists read, think, talk to others, and do experiments. Their investigations often lead to new questions.

In this unit, you will have many chances to think and work like a scientist. How will you find answers to questions you asked?

▶ COMMUNICATING When you communicate, you give information. In science, you communicate by showing results from an activity in an organized way—for example, in a chart. Then you and other people can interpret the results.

▶ HYPOTHESIZING You form a hypothesis when you want to explain how or why something happens. Your hypothesis is an explanation based on what you already know. A hypothesis should be tested in an experiment.

▶ EXPERIMENTING You experiment to test hypotheses. In a test, you must control variables and gather accurate data. You also must interpret the data and draw conclusions.

Are you ready to begin?

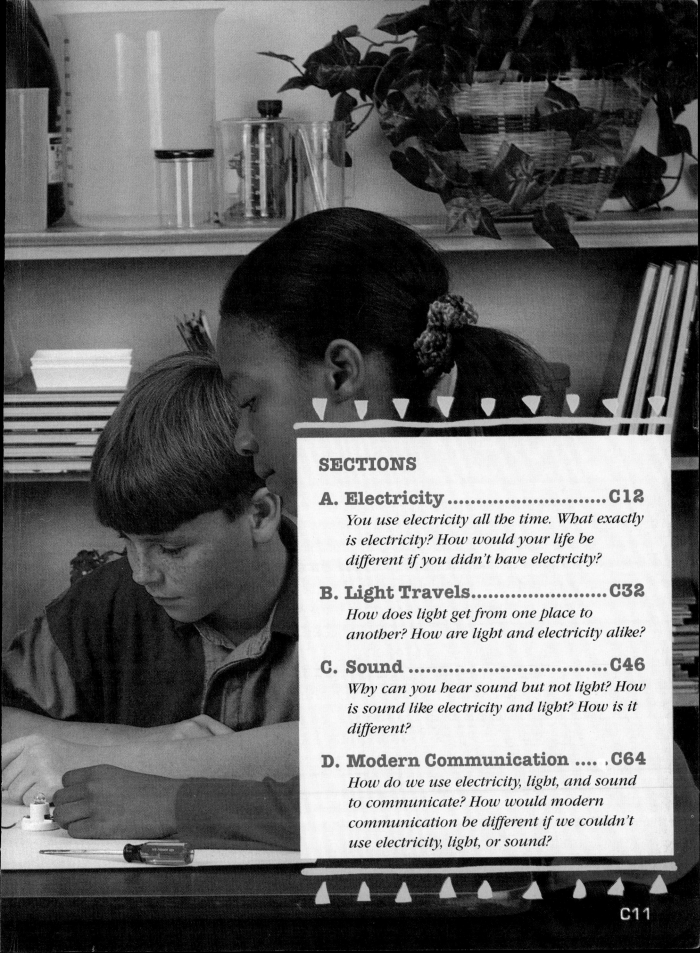

SECTIONS

SECTION A
Electricity

▲ **Fax machine**

You are listening to the radio when the telephone rings. It's a friend who moved away last month, and you are very glad to hear from her. She tells you that her dad's new job allows him to work at home two days a week. He has bought a fax machine so that he can receive important papers from the office.

Electricity was first used for things like electric lights. Today there are many things that require electricity to work. Communication depends a great deal on electricity, as it has ever since the telegraph was invented more than 150 years ago.

In this section, you will explore ideas about electricity and discover how it has improved our ability to communicate.

1 ELECTRIC CHARGES

You probably use electricity to run many things—radios, compact disc players, and televisions, for instance. But did you know that you can use electricity to pick up confetti with a balloon? In this lesson, you will have a chance to see why.

MATERIALS
- balloon
- piece of wool (5 cm x 5 cm)
- confetti
- Science Log data sheet

ACTIVITY

Charge It

By doing the following activity, you will find out some interesting things about balloons.

DO THIS

1 Blow up the balloon so it is completely filled. Tie it closed.

2 Place the confetti on a table. Hold the balloon directly over the confetti. Move the balloon closer and closer to the confetti. Observe what happens. Record your observations.

3 Now rub the balloon with the piece of wool about 20 times. This works best if you rub in only one direction.

4 Hold the rubbed balloon directly over the confetti. Move the balloon closer and closer to the confetti. Record your observations.

THINK AND WRITE

1. Describe what happened to the confetti each time the balloon was held over it.

2. What other materials do you think might interact with the balloon the way the confetti does? Experiment to find out.

Positive and Negative Charges

Even before you experimented with balloons and confetti, you probably experienced similar things. Perhaps you've seen a shirt come out of a clothes dryer with a sock stuck to it. Maybe while taking a sweater off, you pulled it over your head and your hair stood up. You may have walked across a carpeted floor, touched a doorknob, and gotten a shock. All of these things are related. Why do they happen?

It all has to do with electric charges. Every object has electric charges, but they are too small to see. There are two kinds of electric charges. Some charges are positive (+), and some are negative (−). If an object has more positive charges than negative charges, we say that it is *positively charged.* If it has more negative charges than positive charges, we say that it is *negatively charged.* If an object has exactly the same number of positive charges and negative charges, we say that it is *neutral.* Most objects are neutral. They have the same number of positive and negative charges.

Think back to the activity. When the balloon, the wool, and the confetti each had the same number of positive and negative charges, they were neutral. They didn't pull on one another. Then, when you rubbed the balloon with wool, some negative charges moved from the wool to the balloon. The balloon then had extra negative charges. The balloon was negatively charged. The wool was left with a greater number of positive charges—it was positively charged. The confetti was still neutral.

The charged balloon pulled on the neutral confetti, and some of it stuck to the balloon. Charged objects attract neutral objects. The balloon and the wool were attracted to each other. Objects with opposite charges are also attracted to each other.

THINK ABOUT IT

How are charged balloons like magnets? How are they different?

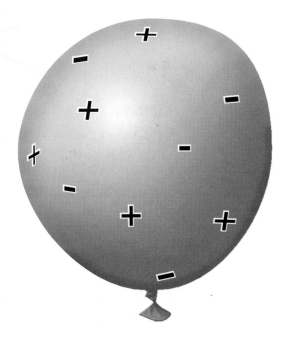

▲ **Neutral balloon**

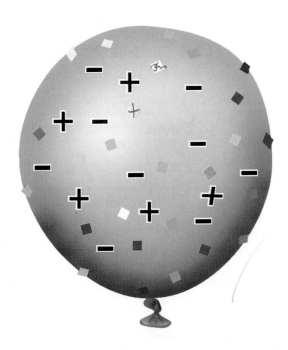

▲ **Charged balloon**

ACTIVITY

Two Charged Balloons

You've seen how a charged balloon attracts uncharged objects. What do you think would happen if two charged balloons were brought together? Try this activity to find out.

DO THIS

❶ Predict whether two charged balloons will attract each other. Write down your prediction.

❷ Blow up the balloons and tie them closed. Tie a piece of thread to each balloon. Tape the threads to a desk or table, so the balloons hang about 5 cm apart.

❸ Rubbing in only one direction, rub both of the balloons with the wool. This will place charges on the balloons. Record what happens to the balloons.

❹ Repeat step 3. This time, put the cardboard between the balloons. Record what happens to the balloons.

THINK AND WRITE

1. Describe what happened to the two balloons.

2. How did placing the cardboard between the two charged balloons affect them? Explain why you think this happened.

Like and Unlike Charges

Look at the photos of two charged balloons. Think about what kind of charges attract, and what kind push away.

◄ Nothing happens when both balloons are neutral—that is, when each balloon has the same number of positive and negative charges.

When you rub the balloons with wool, both balloons gain negative charges. The balloons push away, or repel, each other. That's because they have the same, or like, charges. ▶

◄ Notice what happens when cardboard is placed between the balloons. The cardboard is neutral at first. Then the negative charges on the balloons push the negative charges in the cardboard away from the surface. There are more positive charges near the surface of the cardboard, and the negatively charged balloons are attracted to it.

How do charged balloons relate to your life? Think about when you pull a sweater over your head. The friction, or rubbing, of the sweater charges your hair. Since the strands of hair have the same charge, they repel each other. That's what causes them to stick out.

 This machine generates enough charge to stand this student's hair on end. Doesn't she look like she has just pulled a sweater over her head?

When you walk across a carpet, some of the negative charges from the carpet move to your shoes. These negative charges travel through your body and jump to the metal doorknob when you touch it. You see a spark, and feel the moving charges as a shock. This spark and shock are the result of static electricity. Afterward, the positive and negative charges are equal again.

QUICK CHECK

LESSON 1 REVIEW

1. What do you think would happen if a balloon with a positive charge was brought near a balloon with a negative charge?

2. Explain why a sock and a shirt sometimes cling to each other when they are taken out of a clothes dryer.

2 CURRENT ELECTRICITY

You've seen what happens when electric charges collect in one place. You know that when the charges jump from one object to another, they make a spark. What happens if the charges are constantly moving? In this lesson, you'll have the chance to investigate moving charges.

ACTIVITY

Make It Light

What makes a bulb light? Use a bulb, some wire, and a D-cell to find out.

DO THIS

❶ Use the materials to try to make the bulb light. Do not put the wire directly from one end of the D-cell to the other. That will use up its energy quickly.

❷ Hook up your materials to match the diagrams you are given.

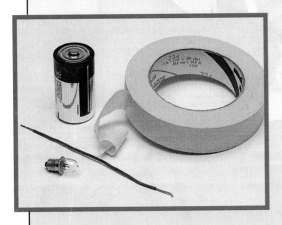

THINK AND WRITE

1. Explain why the bulb did or did not light in each of your tries.

2. What other things can you use in place of the wire? Predict which will work: a rubber band, a strip of aluminum foil, a paper clip, and a paper straw. Test each prediction and record your results.

How Do the Charges Flow?

What did you find out in the last activity?
When did the bulb light?

The bulb lighted only when you made a complete loop called a **circuit.** When the loop was complete, charges could move through the circuit. This flow of charges is called **current electricity.** It got its name because some people thought the charges flowed in the same way that water currents flow in a river.

▲ Look closely at these train tracks. What do you notice about the tracks? Will the train be able to travel all the way around on this track? This is like a *closed* electric circuit. If the circuit is closed or completed, the charges can travel through the circuit.

▲ Now look closely at this track. Will the train be able to travel all the way around it? Why or why not? This is a good model of an electric circuit that is not closed. If an electric circuit is not closed, the charges will not be able to travel through it.

THINK ABOUT IT

If you go home tonight and turn on your bedroom lamp and it lights, what do you know about the circuit it is in ?

ACTIVITY

Make a Switch

After you made the bulb light in the last activity, you had to break the circuit to turn the light bulb off. You removed the wire either from the bulb or from the D-cell. But at home, you don't have to remove a wire. You flip a switch. In this activity, you'll make a switch.

MATERIALS

- 2 metal thumbtacks
- piece of corrugated cardboard (25 x 25 cm)
- paper clip
- 3 bell wires (25 cm with ends stripped)
- D-cell
- battery holder
- 1.5-volt bulb in bulb holder
- Science Log data sheet

DO THIS

1. Push one thumbtack partly into the cardboard. Hook the loop of the paper clip around the thumbtack. Push the tack all the way in as shown.

2. Push the other thumbtack into the cardboard near enough to the first thumbtack so that the paper clip reaches it.

3. Slip the bare ends of one wire under each tack. Press down the tacks to be sure the wires won't slip out.

4. Make a circuit with the paper clip, the wires, the D-cell, and the light bulb.

5. Move the clip so that it touches both thumbtacks. Move the clip so that it touches only one thumbtack.

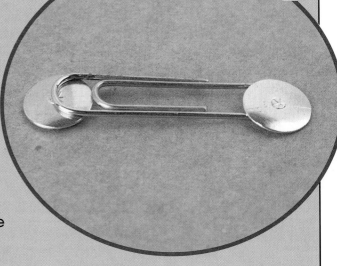

THINK AND WRITE

Write a paragraph that explains how the paper-clip switch works.

Looking Back Where do you use switches in your home? What does a switch do? In this activity, you made a switch. When the switch made a complete circuit between the D-cell and the bulb, the bulb lighted. When the switch was off, the bulb did not light. You can see that a switch is a very useful object.

A Ring of Light

In your home, more than one lamp lights at one time on one circuit. More than one appliance can run at the same time, also. There are two types of circuits that will carry electricity to more than one lamp at a time. But only one type of circuit will continue to carry electricity to other lamps if a bulb burns out in one lamp. See if you can build two kinds of circuits that will light more than one bulb at a time.

Lights in a Row

DO THIS

❶ Using the materials listed, make a circuit that looks just like the one shown. The two bulbs should light.

❷ Predict what will happen if you remove one of the light bulbs. Write down your prediction.

❸ Remove one of the bulbs. Write what happened.

MATERIALS
- 3 bell wires (25 cm with ends stripped)
- 2 bulb holders with bulbs
- D-cell
- battery holder
- Science Log data sheet

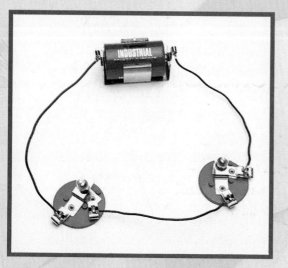

THINK AND WRITE

Why do you think you got the result that you did?

Lights Side by Side

DO THIS

1 Using the materials, make a circuit that looks like the one shown in the diagram. All the bulbs should light.

2 Predict what will happen if you remove one of the bulbs. Write your prediction.

3 Remove one of the bulbs. Record what happened.

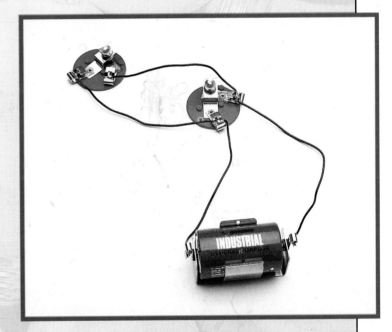

THINK AND WRITE

1. Why do you think you got the result that you did?

2. How could you add a switch to the circuit you just made so that you could turn off both bulbs at once? Draw a diagram to show how you would do it.

Types of Circuits

There is more than one type of circuit. Each type is used in a different way.

The first circuit you made in the activity is called a series circuit. A **series circuit** is a circuit that provides a single path through which electricity can flow. The electricity must flow through each part of the circuit, one after the other.

Have you heard the saying "A chain is only as strong as its weakest link"? A series circuit is like a chain. All it takes is one burned-out bulb or one loose wire to break the circuit. Electricity will stop flowing through the circuit, and none of the lights will work.

The second circuit you made is called a parallel circuit. A **parallel circuit** is a circuit that provides more than one path for electricity to flow through. Each bulb has its own loop. So if one bulb burns out, the other bulbs in the circuit are not affected.

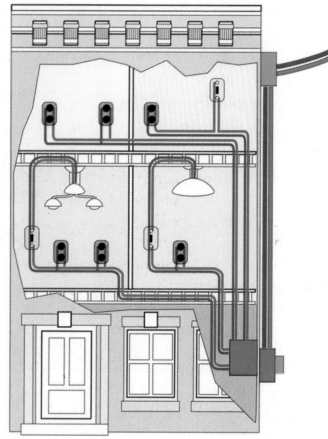

▲ Here are some examples of household circuits.

What would happen if the lights on this bridge were wired in a series? ▼

LESSON 2 REVIEW

Which would be better to use in wiring lights in a home—a series circuit or a parallel circuit? Why?

3 TELEGRAPHS

An electric circuit can be used to do much more than light a bulb. In fact, telegraphs, which are really just simple electric circuits, were used to communicate across the country even before the light bulb was invented. In this lesson, you'll read about the telegraph and have a chance to make one yourself.

Relay Race

It was April 13, 1860. The town of Sacramento, California, was decorated with banners and flags. People in the streets shouted and cheered. Bands played. Bells rang out. A holiday was declared. A new company, the Pony Express, had set a record. In just under ten days, Pony Express

▲ People celebrating the start of the Pony Express

horseback riders had brought news and mail to Sacramento from St. Joseph, Missouri, where the rail lines from the East ended. That was less than half the time it had taken by stagecoach. People were overjoyed. Those who lived in the West no longer felt so far apart from those in the East.

Pony Express riders were like runners in a 2,300-kilometer (about 1,400-mile) relay race. At every 13 to 25 kilometers (10 to 20 miles) along the trail, Pony Express stations were set up. There a rider could take a two-minute break to change horses. Or, if a rider's part of the trip was complete, the saddlebag filled with the mail would be handed to a new rider. Riders and horses could rest, but the mail never stopped.

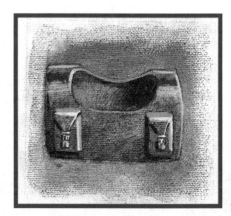

▲ A saddlebag like the ones used by Pony Express riders to carry the mail

The Pony Express riders were heroes to many people. They bravely faced many hazards along the trail. They traveled through blizzards and dust storms. They raced at top speed across deserts, along mountain paths, and through ice-cold streams. They traveled day and night. Their job was to get the mail delivered as quickly as possible.

Despite the dedication of the riders, the Pony Express would not last long. An invention that was little more than an electric circuit and a switch would quickly put it out of business.

The invention was the telegraph patented by Samuel Morse in 1837. It used electricity to send and receive messages in a code called the Morse code.

To send a message, a telegraph operator tapped a handle that worked like a switch. At the receiving end, for each tap of the handle a click would be heard or a pen would draw a dash or a dot. To produce a dot, the operator would hold the handle down for a short time, for about the count of one. To make a dash, the operator would hold it down longer, for about as long as it took to count to three. The dots and dashes of the code stood for the letters of the alphabet. In this way, words could be spelled out.

▲ One of the first messages carried by the Pony Express told of Abraham Lincoln's election as president.

▲ An early telegraph

Samuel Morse developed a code of dots and dashes that stood for letters of the alphabet. This code was used by telegraph operators. ▼

MORSE'S ALPHABET.			
A · —	J · — — —	T —	1 · — — — —
Ä · — · —	K — · —	U · · —	2 · · — — —
B — · · ·	L · — · ·	Ü · · — —	3 · · · — —
C · · — ·	M — —	V · · · —	4 · · · · —
D — · ·	N — ·	W · — —	5 · · · · ·
E ·	O — — —	X — · · —	6 — · · · ·
É · · — · ·	Ö — — — ·	Y — · — —	7 — — · · ·
F · · — ·	P · — — ·	Z — — · ·	8 — — — · ·
G — — ·	Q — — · —	Ch — — — —	9 — — — — ·
H · · · ·	R · — ·		0 — — — — —
I · ·	S · · ·	Understood · · · — · —	

In 1844 the first long-distance telegraph service was set up between Washington, D.C., and Baltimore, Maryland. The first telegraph lines were single wires that often broke.

Even when all of the lines were working, only one message at a time could go through. Bad weather weakened the signals. After a while, people worked out solutions to these problems.

On October 24, 1861, telegraph lines that stretched across the entire United States were completed. News could now travel across the country within hours. Electric wires tied the nation together. Two days later, the Pony Express company went out of business.

▲ A Pony Express rider passing workers stringing telegraph wire

THINK ABOUT IT

You have read about how the telegraph affected the Pony Express. How do you think the invention of the telephone affected the telegraph?

Make an Electromagnet

Samuel Morse's telegraph had a magnet in it, but that magnet was different from the type you use to hang things on your refrigerator. In the following activity, you'll have a chance to make the same type of magnet that was used in Morse's telegraph.

DO THIS

1 Make a data table like the one shown. Fill it in as you work.

HOW MANY PAPER CLIPS WILL AN ELECTROMAGNET PICK UP?			
	Number of Coils		
	10	20	50
Number of Paper Clips			

2 Wrap the wire around the nail to make 10 loops of wire, or coils.

3 Hold the nail over a paper clip. What happens?

4 Attach each end of the wire to the 9-volt battery to make a circuit. Hold the nail over a paper clip. What happens?

5 Use the nail to pick up as many paper clips as you can. Record how many paper clips you can pick up.

6 Disconnect the battery and wrap 10 more loops of wire around the nail. Reconnect the battery. Record how many clips it can pick up now.

7 Repeat step 6 with 50 loops.

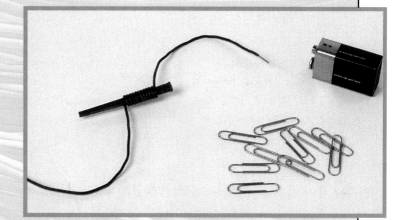

THINK AND WRITE

1. How does the number of coils affect the strength of the electromagnet?

2. Besides changing the number of coils, what else might you do to change the strength of the electromagnet? How could you test your idea?

Looking Back Telegraphs use electromagnets like the one you made in this activity. An **electromagnet** is a kind of magnet that works only when electricity flows through it. As soon as the electricity stops flowing, the magnet can no longer attract certain metals. Electromagnets are much stronger than ordinary magnets.

ACTIVITY

Send a Message

Now that you know how to make an electromagnet, you're ready to build a telegraph.

DO THIS

1 Wrap the middle of the wire around the nail 20 times to make an electromagnet. Leave both ends of the wire free.

2 Bend the tin to form a Z. Use the thumbtack to tack the bottom of the Z to the wood so that its top is almost touching the tip of the electromagnet.

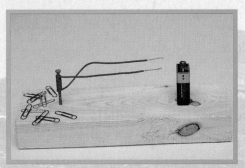

3 Test your telegraph by attaching both ends of the wire to the battery. The electromagnet should pull the tin Z down.

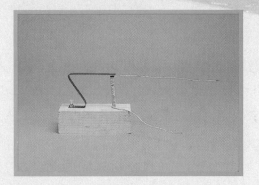

MATERIALS

- piece of wood with nail partly hammered in
- bell wire (45 cm with ends stripped)
- strip of tin (3 cm x 8 cm)
- thumbtack
- 9-volt battery
- paper-clip switch (from the activity on p. C21)
- Teaching Resources p. 92
- Science Log data sheet

4 All you need now is a switch. If you have already made a switch in an earlier activity, you can use it here. If not, the activity on page C21 shows how to make a switch.

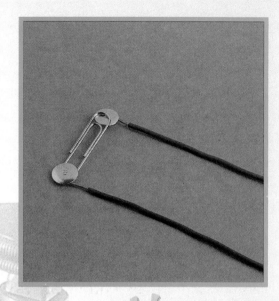

5 Tap the paper clip against the thumbtack to send a short message in Morse code to your partner.

THINK AND WRITE

1. Design a plan for adding a light or bell to your telegraph. Draw a diagram of your plan.

2. **COMMUNICATING** People on the east and west coasts of the United States wanted to communicate more quickly with each other. First they used the Pony Express. Then they used the telegraph, which allowed them to send messages back and forth much more quickly. Why do you think it was important for people to get messages more quickly? Why is fast communication important to scientists?

LESSON 3 REVIEW

1 What does the electromagnet do in a telegraph?

2 Would a regular magnet work as well as an electromagnet in a telegraph? Why or why not?

 DOUBLE CHECK

SECTION A REVIEW

1. Why are many of the circuits in a house parallel circuits and not series circuits?

2. How is an electromagnet similar to a charged balloon? How is it different?

Section B
Light Travels

▲ Laser light show at Stone Mountain, Georgia

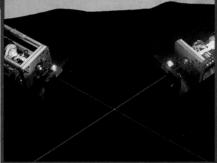

▲ Beams of laser light

Have you ever tried to signal a friend by using a flashlight or a mirror? Light can be used to send signals and messages. Why can light be used in this way? How does light travel? What happens when light hits a mirror?

In this section, you'll have a chance to answer these and other questions about light. As you investigate, keep notes in your Science Log about your questions and the observations you make.

1 WHAT IS LIGHT LIKE?

When you shine a flashlight on an object, why doesn't the light fall on you? Have you ever looked at a wall on a sunny day and noticed a pattern of colored light? Where do the colors come from? In the following pages, you can find answers to questions like these about light.

Light It Up

LIGHT! What is it? Why is it so important to us? When you go into a dark room at night, what is the first thing you do? What would you do if no light came on when you flipped a switch? Think about how you were affected the last time the electricity went out for a few hours.

Electric lights have been used in homes and other buildings only in the last 80 years or so. Before that, people used gas or kerosene lamps.

People have long used the light of fires at night to do the things they needed to do. More than 500 years ago, the Arawak (AHR a wahk) Indians in North America used palm-tree torches. People in Polynesia hung oil-rich nuts together and lighted them. Over 700 years ago in China, people burned lumps of fat on the end of sticks.

THINK ABOUT IT

Write a paragraph about how your life would be affected if the electricity in your neighborhood was off from noon until midnight.

ACTIVITY

How Does Light Travel?

You know that light travels. Light from the sun reaches Earth. The light in your room travels to your book. How does light get from one place to another? Try this activity to find out.

DO THIS

1 Place the index cards in a stack, with the edges even. Using the hole punch, make a hole through the stack of cards.

2 Trace the shape of an index card on both ends of the shoe box. Cut the traced shape out of the ends of the box.

3 Tape the construction paper to the wall. Put a small amount of clay on the desk. Stand one card on edge facing the wall, using the clay to hold the card in place.

4 Put the shoe box over the card, and shine the light through an open end of the box and toward the black paper. Record your observations.

5 Remove the shoe box. Set up another card about 5 cm from the first one, making sure the holes are in line. Shine the light again. What happens?

6 Repeat step 5 with a third and then a fourth card. Record your observations each time.

7 Move one card to the right or left. What happens?

THINK AND WRITE

What did you observe about the light when the holes were in a straight line? What happened when one card was moved? What does this tell you about the way light travels?

A·C·T·I·V·I·T·Y

Bouncing Light

A beam of light travels in a straight line
until it hits something. What happens then?
In the next activity, you'll find out.

DO THIS

1 Stand the book on edge
about 30 cm away from
a wall.

2 Place the eraser on one
side of the book as shown.
Place the ball on the other
side. The eraser and the
book should each be about
30 cm away from the wall.

3 Try to roll the ball so that it
hits the eraser after it hits
the wall.

MATERIALS

- book
- ruler
- chalkboard eraser
- tennis ball
- small mirror
- flashlight
- Science Log data sheet

4 Place the mirror against the wall, directly in front of the book.

5 Place the flashlight where the ball used to be.

6 Shine the light on the eraser by shining the light on the mirror. You can point the flashlight in different directions, but don't pick it up and move it.

THINK AND WRITE

1. What did the ball do when it hit the wall?

2. What happened to the beam of light when it hit the mirror?

Looking Back Beams of light can be reflected. **Reflect** means "to bounce off." Reflected light is what allows you to see yourself in a bathroom mirror. The light bulb over the mirror gives off beams of light. This light bounces off your face and heads toward the mirror. Then it bounces off the mirror and goes into your eyes. That's when you see yourself.

ACTIVITY

The Colors of the Rainbow

You've discovered that light changes direction when it reflects off a mirror. What would happen to light if it passed through an object? In this activity, you'll find out.

DO THIS

1 Tape a piece of white poster board to a wall. Darken the room. Turn on the flashlight and shine it on the poster board. What do you see?

2 Have your partner hold the prism so that one flat side faces down, as shown. The prism should be between you and the poster board. Shine the flashlight on the prism. What do you see on the poster board? Record your observations.

3 Have your partner turn the prism upside down so that the flat side faces up. What happens to the order of the colors? Record your observations.

MATERIALS

- white poster board
- masking tape
- flashlight
- prism
- Science Log data sheet

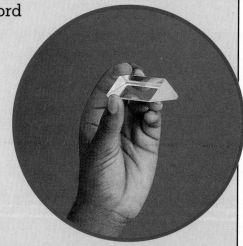

THINK AND WRITE

1. How would you explain what you observed when you turned the prism upside down?

2. How is what you saw like a rainbow? How is a rainbow different? When you see a rainbow, what acts like the prism in this activity?

Looking Back   There are many different colors of light. They all mix together to make white light. When white light passes through a prism, the path of the light bends. The path of some colors of light bends more than the path of others. So when a beam of white light passes through a prism, it spreads apart into bands of different colors.

Spreading Light

Have you ever seen a rainbow? Think about the activity you just did. How do you think a rainbow forms? Look for clues in the poem by David McCord.

THE RAINBOW

by **David McCord**

The rainbow arches in the sky,
But in the earth it ends;
And if you ask the reason why,
They'll tell you "That depends."

It never comes without the rain,
Nor goes without the sun;
And though you try with might
    and main,
You'll never catch me one.

Perhaps you'll see it once a year,
Perhaps you'll say: "No, twice";
But every time it does appear,
It's very clean and nice.

QUICK CHECK

LESSON 1 REVIEW

Write a paragraph explaining how light travels. Make sure you describe the observations you've made in this lesson that support your explanation.

2 EXPLORING LIGHT

You turn lights on and off every day. You've seen lighted candles many times. You know that the sun rises and sets every day. But have you ever really thought about light and some of the things it can do? Now you'll have a chance to do that.

Blocking Light

Think about light hitting a piece of construction paper, a piece of wax paper, and a piece of clear plastic. Which ones let light pass through them? How do you know?

Suppose you and a friend are playing in a room. The sunlight coming in is very bright, and it gets in your eyes. You pull down the shade. Now very little light is coming in, and it's too dark. So you put the shade back up and pull the curtains closed instead. The thin material of the curtains blocks only some of the light. You have just the amount of light you want and can go back to playing a game with your friend.

Light passes through the window glass, the curtains, and the shade in different amounts. Materials you can see through, like glass and water, allow almost all of the light to pass through. Materials that let most light pass through them are **transparent.**

Other materials permit only some light to pass through. Examples of these materials are thin fabrics and frosted glass. Materials that let only some light pass through them are **translucent.**

Light cannot pass through all materials. Some, such as brick, metal, and thick paper, can stop light completely. Since these materials block light, they make shadows. Materials that block light completely are **opaque** (oh PAYK).

THINK ABOUT IT

Look carefully at the two pictures. Why are the shadows of the children different in the pictures?

Classifying Materials

Think of objects you see every day. Which can you see through? Which let only some light through? Which can't you see through at all? Read the activity carefully. Write a hypothesis about how much light will pass through the different types of materials. Test your hypothesis by completing the activity.

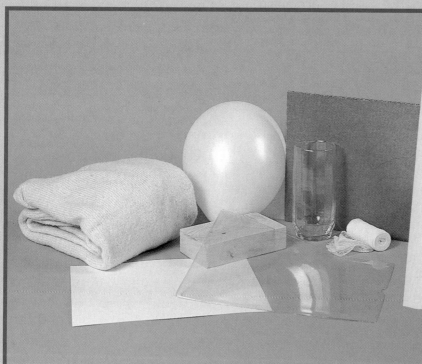

MATERIALS

- block of wood
- flashlight
- white balloon
- measuring tape
- sheet of clear plastic
- piece of gauze
- piece of heavy wool fabric
- sheet of white paper
- piece of cardboard
- Science Log data sheet

DO THIS

1 Place the wood block on a table, one meter from a wall. Point the flashlight toward the wall, and shine the light on the block. Does light pass through the block? Record your observations.

2 Blow up the balloon and tie it closed. Repeat step 1, using the balloon instead of the block. Record your observations.

3 Now, repeat step 1, using the sheet of plastic. Record your observations.

4 Shine the light on each of the other items in the same way. For each item, record what you see.

THINK AND WRITE

1. Classify the items you tested into three groups according to how much light passed through them. Make three columns, using the words *transparent*, *translucent*, and *opaque.*

2. **HYPOTHESIZING** You wrote a hypothesis at the beginning of this activity. Then you tested it. Was your hypothesis correct? Many scientific hypotheses are not correct, but we learn new things from them anyway. If your hypothesis wasn't correct, why wasn't it? Rewrite your hypothesis based on what you know now. Then retest your hypothesis.

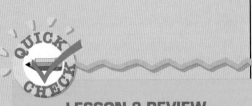

LESSON 2 REVIEW

You may have noticed that many light bulbs are made with "frosted" glass. The glass is white, not clear. How do you think the frosted glass changes the light? Why might a frosted glass bulb be better to use than a clear one?

3 MAKING A PERISCOPE

When people use light to send messages, sending the message is only part of the process. Someone has to receive the message. How would you do that if you were under water in a submarine?

ACTIVITY

MATERIALS
- 1-L milk carton
- ruler
- pen
- scissors
- 2 small mirrors
- Science Log data sheet

Up Periscope

There are many tools that allow us to use light for things other than seeing. In this lesson, you'll use what you know about light to make your own periscope.

DO THIS

❶ Using the ruler as a guide, draw two lines on a side of the carton as shown. The lines should be slightly longer than the width of the mirrors. Cut along each line.

❷ Now draw two lines on the opposite side of the carton. Make sure the lines match the cuts you made. Then cut along each line.

3 Insert the mirrors by sliding them through the cuts in the carton. The mirrors should be placed so that the shiny sides face each other.

4 On the carton, draw a square across from the shiny side of the top mirror. Cut out the square.

5 On the opposite side of the carton, draw a circle the size of a dime. The circle should be across from the shiny side of the bottom mirror. Cut out the circle.

6 Now your periscope is ready. Use it to look over desks and around corners.

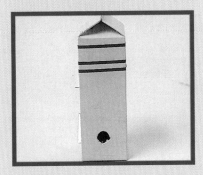

THINK AND WRITE

Draw a diagram of the periscope you made. Label the parts. Then write a paragraph explaining how a periscope works.

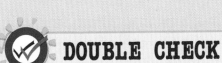

DOUBLE CHECK

SECTION B REVIEW

1. Describe three things that light can do.

2. Describe ways that people use light and its properties to make useful things.

3. A clear object, such as a glass of water, allows most light to pass through it. Does it allow all light to pass through it? How do you know? How could you find out?

QUICK CHECK

LESSON 3 REVIEW

What properties of light allow your periscope to work?

C45

Sound

Listen. Listen to the sounds you hear every day. Sounds bring us messages. The honking horns of cars tell of a traffic jam. The sound of a siren is a warning. The sound of the telephone ringing tells us that someone wants to talk to us. The words we use to speak to one another are sounds. Many of the ways we communicate depend on sound.

In this section, you will explore sound. As you read and do the investigations, keep careful notes in your Science Log. Keeping notes will help you gain a better understanding of what sound is, how it travels, and how you hear it.

1 WHAT IS SOUND?

If a friend asked you if you knew what sound is, you would say, "Of course!" But could you describe sound? Try it. Hard, isn't it? The following activities will help you explore sound. As you do them, you will gain a better understanding of what sound is. Then you will be able to explain it.

What Do You Hear?

You will need: pencil and notebook

When we listen to sounds, we usually pay more attention to what the sounds are than to how they sound. Find a place where you can sit for a while, such as a park or the steps in front of your home or school. Sit quietly and listen to the sounds you hear. As you listen, describe the sounds in your notebook. Don't describe what makes the sound. Describe the sound itself. Is it a high whistling sound or is it low and grumbling? Is it a loud booming sound or a soft rustling sound? After you have finished describing the sounds, share your descriptions with your classmates. See if they can guess what it was you heard.

ACTIVITY

Sounds and Shakes

You probably found it hard to describe the sounds you heard. Now, look at something sound can do.

DO THIS

1 Stretch the plastic wrap over the top of the bowl. Tape the plastic wrap to the bowl, making sure the plastic is as tight around the bowl as it can be.

2 Place the bowl on the table. Put some rice on top of the plastic wrap.

3 Hold the metal pot near the bowl. Watch the rice carefully as you hit the pot with the spoon. Record your observations.

4 Hold the pot about 1 m from the bowl. Gently tap the pot with the spoon. What happens to the rice? Record your observations.

5 Hold the pot near the bowl again, this time without the rice. Lightly rest your finger on the plastic wrap. Have your partner gently tap the pot with the spoon. Then have your partner hit the pot harder. Switch places with your partner and repeat. What did you feel when your finger was on the plastic? What, if any, difference did you feel between the gentle tap and the harder tap? Record your observations.

MATERIALS

- plastic bowl
- plastic wrap
- transparent tape
- uncooked rice
- metal pot
- wooden spoon
- Science Log data sheet

THINK AND WRITE

1. How can sounds make things move? Based on your observations in this activity, write a hypothesis to explain how sound can make things move.

2. How close to the bowl must the pot be in order to make the plastic wrap move?

3. Design another activity to test your answer to question 1.

4. **EXPERIMENTING** All experiments begin with a question. In question 1, you were asked, "How can sounds make things move?" Your answer to this question was a hypothesis that needed to be tested. The only way to test a hypothesis is to conduct an experiment in which you control the variables and collect data. What variables do you need to control in the activity you designed? How would you collect your data?

ACTIVITY

Sound Waves

In the last activity, you saw that sounds can make things shake, or vibrate. But how does sound travel? This activity will give you a chance to investigate this and other questions.

DO THIS

1 Fill the pan with water until it is $\frac{3}{4}$ full.

2 Hit one tuning fork against the rubber eraser. Observe how the tuning fork shakes and listen to the sound it makes when you hold it close to your ear. Then hit the other tuning fork against the eraser and listen to its sound. Compare the sounds of the two tuning forks.

MATERIALS

- clear plastic bowl
- water
- two tuning forks of different notes
- rubber eraser
- Science Log data sheet

3 Hit the first tuning fork against the eraser again. Quickly place the end of the tuning fork into the water at an angle. Be careful not to touch the bottom or sides of the pan. Observe the water.

4 Wait for the water to become still. Then repeat step 3 with the second tuning fork. Observe the water carefully. Were there any differences in the way the water moved with each tuning fork? You may want to repeat steps 3 and 4 to observe the water again.

5 Record your observations.

THINK AND WRITE

1. The way the tuning fork made the water move is similar to the way it makes air move. Based on this information, draw a picture of how you think sound travels.

2. How do you think the sound of a high note differs from that of a low note? Write your conclusion.

Looking Back   How did the tuning fork look after you hit it against the eraser? The tines looked like they were moving back and forth very quickly, didn't they? When you put the tines into the water, the movement produced waves. You made a good model of how sound travels. Back-and-forth vibrations of objects cause waves in the air that travel to your ear. Bones and liquid in your ear transfer the sound waves to your nerves. The nerves change the vibrations into a series of electric impulses that are sent to your brain. Then your brain interprets the sound.

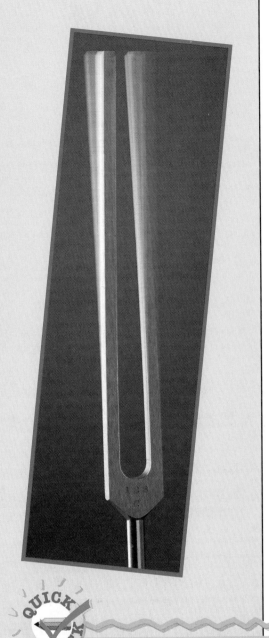

QUICK CHECK

LESSON 1 REVIEW

What observations did you make in the two activities that would lead you to believe that sound travels as a wave?

2 HOW SOUND TRAVELS

Have you ever held your ear against a door to hear something on the other side? Have you ever been swimming and noticed that things sound different when your head is under water? Why do things sound different when sound waves travel through solids, liquids, and gases? In this lesson, you'll have a chance to investigate that question.

ACTIVITY

Sounds in Solids, Liquids, and Gases

Do you think sound travels best through gases (such as air), liquids (such as water), or solids (such as wood or plastic)? Record your predictions.

MATERIALS
- ruler
- tuning fork
- rubber eraser
- water-filled balloon
- Science Log data sheet

DO THIS CAUTION

1 Stand next to your partner, with your back turned. Have your partner strike the tuning fork on the eraser, and hold the tuning fork about 10 cm from your ear. Listen carefully to the sound. Switch places with your partner, and repeat this step.

② Put your head down on your desk and hold your ear against the desktop. Have your partner strike the tuning fork on the eraser and touch the handle of it to the desktop about 20 cm from your ear. Listen carefully to the sound. Switch places with your partner and repeat this step.

③ **CAUTION: Do not break the balloon with the tuning fork.** Place the water-filled balloon at the edge of a table. Put your ear against the balloon. Have your partner strike the tuning fork on the eraser, and gently touch the handle of it to the balloon. Listen carefully to the sound. Switch places with your partner and repeat this step.

④ Discuss your observations with your partner. When was the sound loudest? Record your observations and conclusions.

THINK AND WRITE

1. Use your observations to write a paragraph comparing how the sounds traveled through air, wood, and water.

2. **HYPOTHESIZING** Based on what you discovered in this activity, form a hypothesis about where sound travels best. How could you test your hypothesis? Test it and write a paragraph about the results. Was your hypothesis supported? It's OK if it wasn't. Scientists often make hypotheses that aren't supported.

Evelyn Glennie Percussionist

If you were going to play a musical instrument, which of your senses would you use the most? Read on to see if Evelyn Glennie agrees with you.

In a large symphony hall, an orchestra fills the room with music. Clarinets, violins, flutes, cellos, basses, and drums all play together to create a wonderful sound. In the back of the orchestra, playing the drums, is Evelyn Glennie. Like the other musicians, Glennie has spent long, hard hours practicing her skills. Unlike the other musicians, Glennie is deaf.

Glennie does not hear music the way a hearing person does. She "hears" it in other ways—by reading the music from the score and by feeling it with her body.

Evelyn Glennie grew up on her family's farm in Scotland. She was born hearing, and as a young child enjoyed music. As many children do, she studied piano, clarinet, and percussion instruments. Percussion instruments include drums, maracas (muh RAH kuhz), cymbals (SIM buhlz), and other instruments that make a sound by being struck, shaken, or scraped.

As Glennie grew older, she began to lose her hearing because of an illness. Because Glennie loved music so much, she did not let her hearing loss stop her from continuing to play musical instruments.

▼ **Colorado Symphony Orchestra**

▲ **Evelyn Glennie**

She felt that her way of "hearing" music was far better than the way she had heard it as a young child. She felt that she had a unique way of experiencing music.

Glennie studied music at the Royal Academy of Music in London and graduated with honors. Since then, she has appeared in many concerts, played with the Colorado Symphony Orchestra, and made several records.

Glennie does not practice for a concert the same way other musicians do. First, she studies the music and does careful planning. "A lot of my practice is done silently, away from the instruments," she says. "I'm very, very aware of the room I'm playing in." Glennie asks questions about the room she will be playing in so she will know how sound travels in the room.

When Glennie plays music, she feels the sound vibrations through her hands, her body, and her feet. Many of these vibrations are transmitted through the floor. For this reason, Glennie often works barefoot.

For Glennie, deafness is not an obstacle. "At the end of the day, I'm just a musician," she says. "I just speak through music."

▼ **Practicing with the symphony**

QUICK CHECK

LESSON 2 REVIEW

❶ Where would it be easier for Evelyn Glennie to perform as part of an orchestra—in a room with wooden floors or in one that is carpeted? Why?

❷ Telephones allow people to communicate over long distances. Many whales can do this without using telephones. How do they communicate when they are far apart?

3 MAKING AND HEARING SOUNDS

You've seen that sound waves cause things to vibrate and that things that vibrate can produce sound waves. Sometimes it's easy to see how this happens — a guitar string vibrates when you play it, and loud music can make the glasses on a table shake. But sometimes the way sound works isn't so easy to see. For example, how can a stereo speaker sound like an entire band in concert? Also, how do we hear sound waves? In this lesson, you will have a chance to answer these questions about making and hearing sounds.

ACTIVITY

Loud and Soft

Ssh! The baby's sleeping. What can you learn about loud and soft sounds? Try this activity to find out.

MATERIALS

- safety goggles
- 5 rubber bands of different lengths and thicknesses
- shoe box
- Science Log data sheet

DO THIS

1. **CAUTION: Use care in stretching each rubber band.** Put on the safety goggles.

2. Wrap the widest rubber band around the shoe box as shown.

❸ Pluck the rubber band lightly. What do you hear?

❹ Pluck the rubber band harder. What do you notice about the noise it makes?

❺ Record your observations.

❻ Repeat steps 2–5 with the rest of the rubber bands.

THINK AND WRITE

1. How was the sound produced when you plucked the rubber bands?

2. How did the sound change as you plucked harder?

3. What other objects can you think of that produce sounds in the way that the rubber bands do?

4. If you wanted to form a rubber-band musical group, what would you need to do? Try out your ideas.

Making Sounds Louder

"Speak up. I can't hear you," said the teacher. What did the teacher want you to do? Do this activity to find out.

DO THIS

1 Strike the tuning fork on the eraser. Pay close attention to how loud a sound the tuning fork makes.

2 Strike the tuning fork again. While it is vibrating, hold it on your desktop. How loud is the sound?

3 Roll a piece of construction paper to form a cone. Then cut off the point about 4 cm from the tip. Tape the seam. Now you have a megaphone with an opening at both ends.

MATERIALS

- tuning fork
- rubber eraser
- sheet of construction paper
- ruler
- scissors
- masking tape
- straight pin
- paper cup
- record turntable
- old phonograph record
- Science Log data sheet

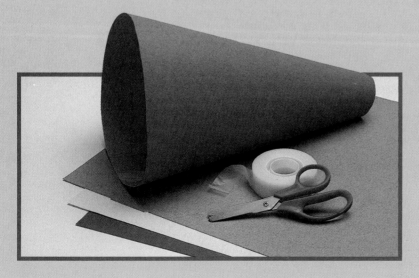

4 Stand about 1 m from your partner. Call his or her name in a normal voice. Then put the megaphone to your mouth and call him or her again. Have your partner take the cone and do the same. When was the sound louder?

5 Push the straight pin into the center of the bottom of the paper cup from the inside as shown.

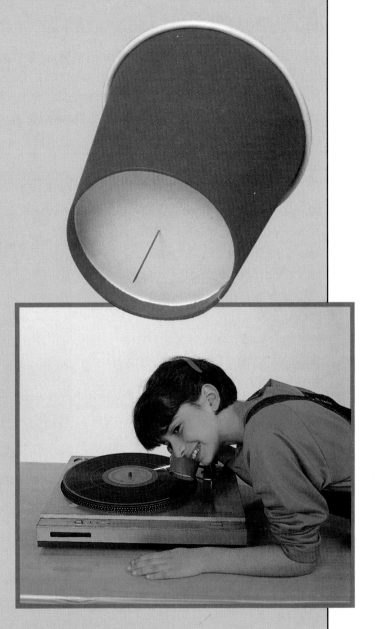

6 Put the record on the turntable. Give the turntable a push with your hand to get it spinning.

7 Hold the cup lightly in your hand. Touch the tip of the pin to the grooves of the record as it spins. Put your ear close to the open end of the cup. What do you hear? Look at the point of the pin. What happens to it as the record goes around?

THINK AND WRITE

Write a paragraph explaining what you heard in the paper cup and why. How can you make sounds louder?

How Do We Hear a Record Player?

When you held the tuning fork against your desk, the tuning fork made the desktop vibrate. Since the desktop is much larger than the tuning fork, it made the air vibrate more. The vibrating air made the sound louder.

Along the grooves of a record are tiny bumps. When the pin rode in the groove, it hit these bumps and vibrated. The cup vibrated as well. Since the cup has a larger surface than the needle, it moved more air when it vibrated. Thus, the sound was louder.

The shape of the cup also helped make the music sound louder. Sound waves bounced off the side of the cup and out the open end. The same thing happened when you called your partner while using the cone. Without the cone, the sound waves traveled in all directions. With the cone, more sound waves were directed toward your partner.

But how did your partner hear the sounds? To answer that question, you need to understand how the ear works.

Record player ▼

A close-up of record grooves ▶

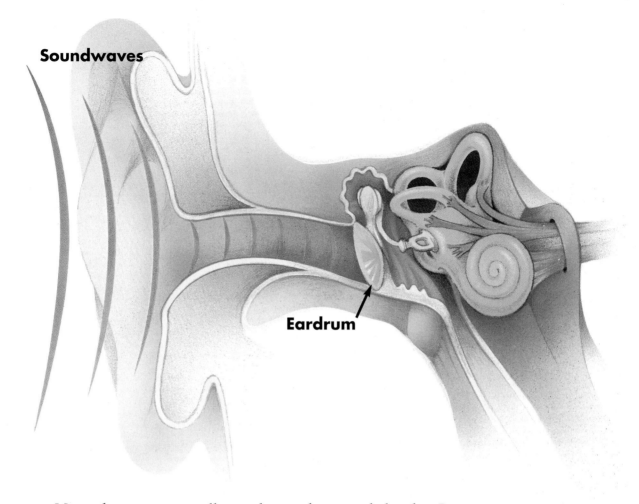

Soundwaves

Eardrum

Megaphones are usually used to make sounds louder. But you can also use them to hear better. In fact, you actually have "megaphones" on your head—your ears. Here's how the human ear works.

As sound waves move through the air, they hit the outer ear. The sound waves bounce off the outer ear. Since the outer ear has a cone-like shape, the sound waves are directed into the ear.

There, they hit a thin circle of tissue called an *eardrum*. When the sound waves hit the eardrum, it vibrates and sends signals through the nerves to the brain. The brain interprets the signals as sounds.

THINK ABOUT IT

Why do you sometimes see people put their hands behind their ears and cup their hands?

Animal Ears and Sonar

The ears of many animals are shaped differently from ours, but they work the same way ours do.

Look at the length of the jack rabbit's ears. How do its long ears help it to hear? Talk this over with your neighbor. ▼

▲ This fox can hear sounds much farther away than it can see objects. Sharp hearing is an adaptation. How is this adaptation useful for hunting prey?

A cat can move its ears around to pick up very soft sounds. Cats hunt birds, moles, and mice for food. Think about the sounds these animals make. Now you can see why cats need to have good hearing. ▼

Bats make use of sound in an unusual way. This bat is a night hunter, but it has difficulty seeing its prey. Instead, when it goes hunting, it makes quick, high-pitched squeaks. In fact, the squeaks are so high that humans can't hear them. If the sound waves of the squeaks hit an insect, they bounce back as an echo does. The bat hears where the echo is coming from and zooms in on the insect. ▶

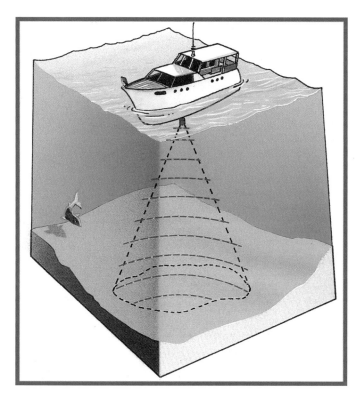

◀ Ships use sound in much the same way bats do to detect objects underwater. Their sonar equipment sends out sounds. If the sound waves hit something, an echo bounces back. The sonar equipment records these sounds, and the sonar operator can then tell from the echo where the objects are underwater.

QUICK CHECK

LESSON 3 REVIEW

Describe the process that allows you to hear a person clapping.

DOUBLE CHECK

SECTION C REVIEW

When Native Americans hunted buffalo for food, they needed to know if the herds were near. In order to find out, they would sometimes put their ears to the ground. Explain why they would have done this.

SECTION D
Modern Communication

▲ Cave painting showing a pony in the snow

▲ Cuneiform tablet

People have communicated in many ways throughout history. They have painted pictures on rocks or animal skins to tell stories. They have used drum or smoke signals as a code to warn of danger or to share news. In time, alphabets were invented so that words could be written down.

Today we communicate in many different ways, using inventions that include telephones, computers, and fax machines. You probably use at least one of these inventions every day. Have you ever wondered how they work? In this section, you will find out.

1 COMPUTERS

You can play basketball, build a house, explore new territory, or travel around the world—and never leave your chair. All of these activities can be done at a computer.

The Development of Computers

In this unit, you have read about some of the ways people communicate. Now let's look at a fairly new invention—the computer.

In the nineteenth century, Pony Express riders delivered messages over long distances, riding as fast as their horses could go. As quick as the Pony Express riders were, however, the telegraph was much quicker. The telegraph used electric current and a code to send messages to and receive them from distant places.

People continued to want to receive and process information as quickly as possible. In 1946 a breakthrough occurred—the first computer was invented. However, the first computer didn't look anything like the ones in use today.

The first computer was very large. In fact, it filled a whole room. This computer was called *ENIAC*, which stood for *E*lectronic *N*umerical *I*ntegrator *a*nd *C*omputer. What that meant was that it was a machine that processed numbers. It did much the same thing that a hand-held calculator does today. ENIAC did not have a memory, so it could not store a program. But ENIAC was fast—at least it was fast compared to paper-and-pencil calculation. It could multiply 333 ten-digit numbers a second.

▲ **ENIAC**

ENIAC worked by using electric current. But back then, large tubes and miles of wire were needed to construct the electric circuits. Before a calculation could be done, thousands of switches had to be set and many cables had to be plugged in.

There were some problems with ENIAC. The tubes that were used to build it gave off a tremendous amount of heat. Today that wouldn't be a big problem because we could just cool the room with air conditioning. In 1946, however, air conditioning wasn't in use. The room that held ENIAC was cooled by fans. Unfortunately, the fans couldn't keep the equipment cool enough, so the computer broke down frequently.

▲ **Vacuum tube**

In the 1950s, improvements were made in technology. The tubes were replaced by transistors that were smaller and did not break down as easily. This allowed computers to become smaller and easier to use. Businesses began buying computers, which were now about the size of a refrigerator. These computers had to be kept in air-conditioned rooms because they would break down if they got too hot. These computers still could only process numbers. They did not have the ability to display images on a screen.

Today you can pack a computer in a briefcase. You can find even smaller computers inside things like microwave ovens and hand-held games. Computers are much less expensive to buy, and they don't break down very often. They are also much faster than ENIAC was. As a result, there are many more computers in use today.

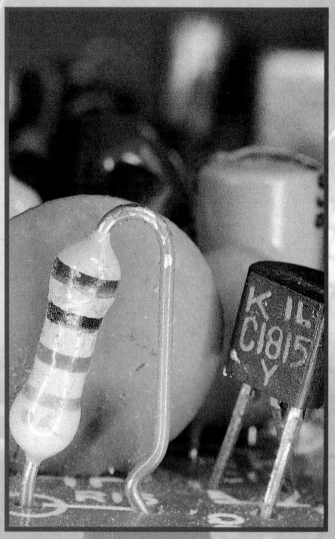

▲ Transistor

THINK ABOUT IT

Where and how do you use computers?

ACTIVITY

A Finger Computer

Computers can be used to calculate a huge amount of mathematical information in what seems like an instant. Have you ever wondered how computers can calculate so quickly? Do this activity to get an idea of how computers work.

MATERIALS

- 4 pieces of masking tape (2.5 cm)
- marking pen
- Science Log data sheet

DO THIS

1 Draw a chart like the one shown.

2 Place one piece of tape around the fingernail of your little finger on your right hand. Write the number 1 on the tape.

3 Place the second piece of tape around the index finger of your right hand. Write the number 2 on the tape.

4 Place the third piece of tape around the index finger of your left hand. Write the number 4 on the tape.

5 Place the last piece of tape around the little finger of your left hand. Write the number 8 on the tape.

Number	Fingers Used
1	
2	
3	
4	
5	
6	
7	
8	
9	
10	
11	
12	
13	
14	
15	

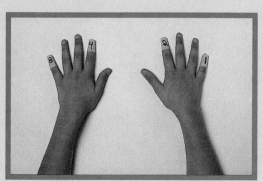

6 Place your hands—palms down—on your desk. Curl your fingers under.

7 You will now use your fingers as a computer. To do this, remember this rule: A finger that is pointing out stands for the number marked on it. A finger that is curled under stands for zero. For example, to show zero, all four marked fingers are folded under. To show 1, the finger marked 1 is pointed out. To show 3, both the finger marked 1 and the finger marked 2 are pointed out (2 + 1 = 3). The other fingers remain under.

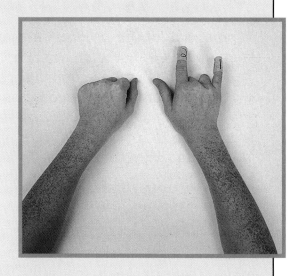

8 Now use your finger computer to show each number in your chart. You must put out fingers that add up to the number. You may not use any finger more than once for each number.

9 Record in your chart which fingers you used to make each number.

THINK AND WRITE

1. How did you show numbers in this activity?

2. COMMUNICATING When you communicate, you share information. How have computers changed the ways we communicate?

Looking Back A computer contains many electric circuits. Information travels in a computer as electric current. Just like a telegraph, a computer has parts inside it that act as switches. These switches can be turned on or off. When these switches are turned on or off, the computer can show numbers just as you did with your finger computer. As a matter of fact, by using only 20 switches, a computer can count to over one million.

Make It Smaller

Almost half of the children in the United States use a computer at home or at school. Almost 27 million American homes have computers.

How did computers become as small, fast, and inexpensive as they are? What technologies have allowed us to make computers so common and useful? As you do the activities that follow, you will find out.

Recall that the first computer was so large that it filled a room. Then when smaller parts, like the transistor, were invented, the computer became smaller. But it was still the size of a refrigerator! Now you can wear a computer on your wrist. That's right—watches that have calculators built in or that can store telephone numbers are a type of computer. This small size is made possible by the silicon (SIL uh kahn) chip. Silicon is a chemical found in sand and certain types of rocks. What is important about silicon is the way electricity can travel through it. The surface of a silicon chip can be treated so that electricity will travel very quickly through some areas and won't travel at all through other areas. This allows complicated electric circuits to be constructed on very small chips. These pictures show some inventions that have been made possible because of the silicon chip.

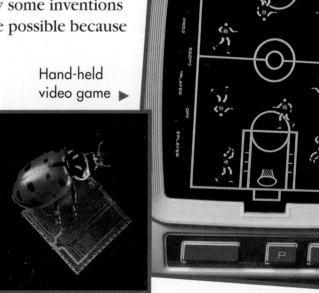

Hand-held video game ▶

Computer chip ▶

Digital watches can have calculators built into them. Think how handy this would be if you were in a store and wanted to calculate the sale price of an electronic game you wanted to buy. ▶

◀ The first computer was as large as a room and could only perform the processes that had been done on an adding machine. However, it did them much faster. Advances in technology since 1946 allow people to use powerful computers that can fit on their laps. Also, they do much more than compute mathematical numbers. They are able to accept and store information that can then be printed on paper or sent from one place to another over telephone lines. Who knows what the future will bring to the computer industry?

THINK ABOUT IT

1. Name two other inventions that might use silicon chips.

2. Why is it important that a computer's electric circuits be made on such a small chip? Why is speed so important?

Break the Code

Early computers were invented to *compute,* that is, to do mathematical calculations. They began to take the place of instruments like the abacus (AB uh kuhs), the slide rule, and the adding machine. But is computing all they do now?

The advantage of using computers was that they could do large numbers of complicated calculations very quickly. As computers began to get smaller, it became possible to use them in more places. Because of this, people began to look for new ways to use the computer. In time, a way to process words with a computer was developed.

In order to allow the computer to process words, a new code was developed and agreed on. Look at the chart on the next page to see how the code works. Each letter of the alphabet is represented by an eight-digit code. Each digit is either a zero or a one. This is called a *binary* (BY nuhr ree) *code.* The word *binary* means "two."

Abacus ▶

▼ Old fashioned adding machine

▲ Slide rules were used to make complicated calculations.

THINK ABOUT IT

How did developing a computer that could understand letters change how computers are used?

A C T I V I T Y

Using a Binary Code

How do computers use the binary code to process words? Do this activity to find out.

MATERIALS
• Science Log data sheet

DO THIS

❶ Place your hands palms down on your desk. Using four fingers on each hand (do not use your thumbs), do the following: Curl your fingers under. Now all of your fingers stand for zeros. If you want a finger to stand for the digit 1, point it outward. You can now signal the code by using your fingers and the code chart. For example, the code for the letter a is 11100001.

❷ Find the letters for your first name on the code chart. Write down the code for your name. Use your fingers to "signal" your name.

❸ Decode the following message, and write it down. Read across the page.

11111001	11101111	11110101	11100100
11101001	11100100	11101001	11110100

a	11100001
b	11100010
c	11100011
d	11100100
e	11100101
f	11100110
g	11100111
h	11101000
i	11101001
j	11101010
k	11101011
l	11101100
m	11101101
n	11101110
o	11101111
p	11110000
q	11110001
r	11110010
s	11110011
t	11110100
u	11110101
v	11110110
w	11110111
x	11111000
y	11111001
z	11111010

THINK AND WRITE

1. How is the code you just used similar to Morse code?

2. Why do you think binary code is ideal for use with an electric switch?

3. Make up a message, and use binary code to send it to a friend.

QUICK CHECK

LESSON 1 REVIEW

How are a telegraph and a computer alike? How are they different?

2 COMMUNICATION ACROSS DISTANCES

Sound, light, and electricity are used in many inventions we use to communicate. We use these devices without thinking much about them. If the telephone rings, we answer it, speak to the caller, and then hang up. We don't give much thought to how the telephone works or to the different ways it can be used. But there are new uses of the telephone and other inventions that are very exciting. Now you'll have a chance to investigate some of these.

ACTIVITY

A Paper-Cup Telephone

You can make a simple model of a telephone that doesn't need electricity.

DO THIS

❶ Use a pencil to poke a small hole in the bottom of each cup.

MATERIALS
- 2 large paper cups
- sharpened pencil
- string (2 m)
- 2 toothpicks
- Science Log data sheet

2 Push one end of the string through the hole in the bottom of one of the cups. Be sure to push the string from the outside to the inside.

3 Tie the free end of the string to a toothpick. You may need to break the toothpick if it is too long.

4 Repeat steps 2 and 3 with the other end of the string and the second cup.

5 Keep one end of the "telephone," and give the other to your partner. Stretch the string tight.

6 To use the telephone, one person speaks into a cup while the other person puts the other cup up to his or her ear and listens. Speak back and forth to see how well your "telephone" works.

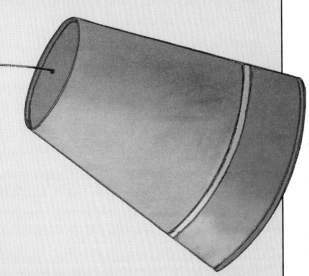

THINK AND WRITE

1. How does sound travel in your paper-cup phone?

2. **EXPERIMENTING** All experiments begin with a question. Suppose you wanted to find the answer to the question "Which material makes the best connector in a paper-cup telephone?" You would need to write a hypothesis, design a test, and carry it out. Then you would collect data, organize it, and draw a conclusion. Work with a partner to write down the steps you would follow to answer that question.

How the Telephone Works

You have just made your own paper-cup "telephone." Although it does work to send voice messages over short distances, it would not work very well over long distances. It also wouldn't be a very good system for linking large numbers of people.

In 1876 Alexander Graham Bell invented a telephone that was the model for the phones we use today. By the early 1900s, telephone use had become more common, and many wires were needed to connect the existing telephones. At first these wires were run above ground on poles. But as the telephone became more and more popular, the mass of wires became huge. Imagine what would have happened if a storm had knocked down the telephone wires for a neighborhood, a city, or even an entire state! To prevent this, many areas began to bury the wires underground in bundles called *cables*. Each cable can hold up to 2,700 pairs of wires.

▲ Old-fashioned crank telephone

▲ In some areas, telephone cables are strung on poles.

Telephone wires carry electric current. When a person speaks into the mouthpiece of the telephone, his or her voice changes the strength of the electric current traveling across the wires. When the electric current reaches the receiver at the other end, it is changed back into sound by an electromagnet. The changes in strength of the electric current coming into the electromagnet cause a part of the electromagnet to vibrate back and forth. This sends sound vibrations to the ear of the listener.

When the telephone rings, it signals that a call is coming in. When you pick up the receiver, the plunger pops up. The plunger, or *switchhook*, is really a switch. When it pops up, it completes the circuit and lets electricity pass through. When you hang up, the handset pushes the switchhook down and the circuit is broken.

▲ The large telephone cable is made of wires. The small telephone cable is made of glass. Each cable can carry the same number of calls.

Switchhook

Receiver

THINK ABOUT IT

Why do you think a paper-cup telephone would not work well over long distances or for connecting large numbers of people?

Send a Fax

Telephone lines were designed to carry voice messages. But as technology improved and changed, ways to carry other types of information along telephone lines were developed.

Communicating by means of a facsimile (fak SIM uh lee), or fax, machine has become more and more common. You have seen how binary code can be used to send messages that contain words. Now find out how binary code can be used to communicate by sending pictures.

▲ **Fax machine**

DO THIS

1 Keep one end of the paper-cup telephone and give the other to your partner.

2 Mark off a space 10 squares by 10 squares on the graph paper. Draw a simple picture by filling in some of the squares on the graph paper. Each square must be either completely filled in or completely blank.

MATERIALS
- paper-cup telephone
- graph paper
- Science Log data sheet

❸ Write the binary code for your picture. Begin with the top line of boxes on the left-hand side. If the first box is filled in, write down a 1 on the sheet of paper. If the box is not filled in, write down a zero. Repeat this step for all the other boxes in the row. Write the code for all the rows.

Send the Fax.
0000110000

❹ Now read the completed code to your partner, line by line, using the paper-cup phone. Your "receiver" should write down the code, line by line, on a piece of paper.

❺ The receiver should now use the code to draw a picture on graph paper. If the first number is a 1, he or she fills in the first box on the first line. If the number is a zero, the box should be left blank.

❻ Compare the receiver's drawing with the drawing you sent. In other words, compare the "faxed" copy with the original.

THINK AND WRITE

A facsimile is not an actual copy. What do you think the difference is between a facsimile and a photocopy?

Looking Back A fax machine looks at a picture as if it were made up of thousands of dots. The machine translates the dark places (dots) and light places (no dots) into binary code. This code is sent over the telephone wires to another fax machine. A printer inside the receiving fax machine prints a dot wherever the original picture is dark. The darker it is, the more dots are printed. This builds up a copy of the original picture.

Signals Without Wires

Sometimes you need to send messages, but you don't have wires. Can it be done? Read on to find out.

It is not always necessary to use a wire to send a signal. *Radio waves* are bursts of energy created by electromagnets. These bursts can be sent from one antenna to another through the air. Radio waves are used to send signals that bring you the music and news you listen to on your radio at home or in your car. Radio waves are also used to carry signals between cellular phones. This is why we can have portable telephones as well as telephones in cars and on airplanes. These telephones are not connected to telephone cables.

Car phones are fairly common these days. ▼

◄ You can even call home from an airplane.

▲ Making phone calls from the backyard—no problem.

Some telephone signals are transmitted by microwaves. These bursts of energy are similar to the ones used in a microwave oven, but not as powerful. For communications, microwave signals are sent from tower to tower across long distances.

Microwave transmission towers transfer signals that enable us to make phone calls without wires. ▶

Each microwave tower has a dish-shaped antenna to catch the signal and pass it on to the next tower. Each tower is about 50 kilometers (30 miles) from the next. Tens of thousands of these towers are located all over the United States. But microwave towers cannot be built over oceans. So how are signals sent across the ocean? They used to be sent along cables under the water. But today they are sent to a satellite in space! The satellite then bounces the signal back to Earth on the other side of the ocean.

▲ Satellites relay signals all over the world.

▲ Satellite dishes receive the signals relayed by satellites.

QUICK CHECK

LESSON 2 REVIEW

❶ Why do you think microwave towers are located about 50 kilometers (30 miles) apart rather than about 500 kilometers (300 miles)?

❷ Why would using satellites to transmit signals be better than using underwater cables?

3 THE FUTURE OF COMMUNICATION

As you have read, many improvements have been made in communication since the days of the Pony Express. What lies ahead? What new inventions are being worked on? What will communication be like in the next century? Read the following article for a peek at the future.

VIRTUAL REALITY

Computers Create Lifelike Worlds You Can Step Into

by **Brianna Politzer**
from *3-2-1 Contact*

LITERATURE

You're sitting in your living room, playing a video game. You pull the joystick to the left, and the plane you're flying swoops over a river valley.

Suddenly—zap!!—you blink your eyes and you're no longer in the room, but sitting inside the cockpit of the plane. You see the dark purple mountains on either side of you, the river below, the clouds above. You hear the wind rushing over the wings, the hum of the engine. You no longer need the joystick. To fly higher, you look upward. By simply moving your head, you send the plane left or right.

Sounds like a science-fiction movie, right? Wrong!

New computer technology makes it possible to experience flying a plane, traveling through space or even visiting imaginary worlds—without ever leaving the room. Scientists call it virtual reality,

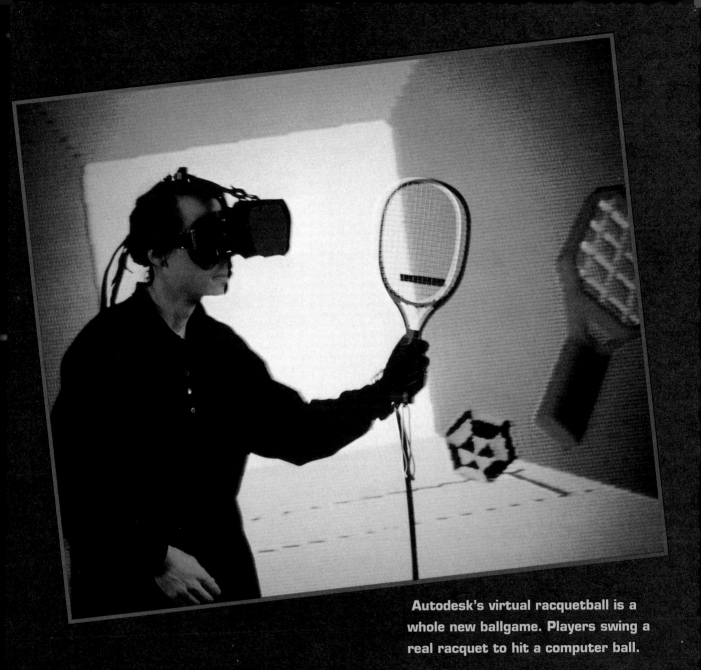

Autodesk's virtual racquetball is a whole new ballgame. Players swing a real racquet to hit a computer ball.

because it feels so close to being real.

With virtual reality (or artificial reality, as it's sometimes known), the user wears a special glove called a data glove and a pair of goggles. Inside the glove and goggles are tiny electronic sensors. When you move your head or your hand, the sensors tell the computer to respond. (This is how you controlled the plane's movements.)

The computer interprets your movements as commands. In a virtual world, you reach your hand toward an object and close your fingers. The computer understands the motion as a command to pick up the object.

The goggles make virtual reality

Jaron Lanier, founder of VPL, thinks virtual reality allows people to interact better. Some critics think it will keep people apart and in their own worlds.

more…real. In each eyepiece of the goggles is a tiny computer screen that displays a computer image. The image on each screen is slightly different. When you see both screens at the same time, the image looks three-dimensional. It's so lifelike, it's almost like being there.

Is It Live or…?

"It feels like you're inside a cartoon," says Jaron Lanier. A pioneer in artificial reality, Lanier is the head of a company called VPL in Redwood City, California. VPL makes gloves and goggles for virtual reality programs. "Everything feels real, although it doesn't quite seem natural."

In one project Lanier is working on, you put on gloves and goggles and step into a world where there are strange vines and bushes growing everywhere. "When you pick up the plants, they change shape and make music," Lanier says.

In another virtual world, created by scientists at a company called Autodesk in Sausalito, California, you sit on a real bicycle, put on goggles and begin to pedal. As you pedal faster, something incredible happens: It seems as if the bicycle is rising into the air. Soon, you feel you're flying above the Earth, just like the kids in *E.T.*

"It's like being in a dream, a vivid dream," says Randal Walser, a scientist at Autodesk. "You feel as if your entire self is in another place."

Autodesk has also developed a virtual reality racquetball game. Two people play together. Both see the imaginary ball and their imaginary racquets. They control their racquets by the motion of their gloved hands. They even hear a "thwack!" as the racquet hits the ball.

Sometimes artificial reality can be produced without gloves and goggles. This happens at an exhibit called "Videoplace" at the Connecticut State Museum of Natural History. Visitors stand in front of a screen. Below the screen is a video camera. Walk in front of the camera and your shadow appears on the screen.

As you face the shadow, a strange green, insect-like creature darts onto the screen and dances on the shadow's head. Hold out your hands and the creature crawls onto the shadow's fingers. Capture the creature between the shadow hands and it explodes!

In another game at Videoplace (games are changed by walking away from the camera, then walking back in front of it), a person's finger leaves different-colored trails on the screen.

At Videoplace, visitors can light up the skyline just by pointing a finger.

When all five fingers are spread out, the trails disappear, as if a chalkboard had been erased. o

These and other games at Videoplace are made possible by 14 separate computers. Each computer is connected to the video camera, explains Myron Krueger, the exhibit's inventor.

"The computers analyze your silhouette 30 times every second," says Krueger. "It can tell what part of your body is where on the screen. If you hold up one finger, the computer knows that it's one finger. If you hold up all five fingers, the computer also knows that."

Inside the Body

But virtual reality isn't all fun and games. The technology has serious uses, too.

Scientists are now making virtual reality programs that allow a surgeon to travel inside an enlarged, three-dimensional computer image of a patient's body. The graphics are made from very detailed pictures similar to X-rays. If a patient had a cancerous tumor, for example, a surgeon could travel inside a picture of his body to get a better view of how to operate.

Architects are even strolling through virtual reality buildings. If they don't like the way things are laid out, they can change the building *before* it's actually built.

And in Japan, a company uses virtual reality to sell its kitchens. Before ordering a real kitchen, customers walk through a virtual version, opening virtual cabinets and checking out virtual appliances. They can even pick up virtual dishes— carefully. If dropped, they'll "virtually" break!

Future air traffic controllers may direct planes with the movement of a gloved hand.

The Power Glove brings virtual reality to video games.

Perhaps the most exciting use of virtual reality is to get a bird's-eye view of planets and galaxies. Users of a virtual reality project at NASA—the U.S. space agency—can "fly" through outer space.

Spaced Out

Michael McNeill, a scientist at the University of Illinois, is helping NASA with this project. "You really feel like you're floating in space," he says. "You move around, in and out, just by moving your head. It's much different from just looking into a computer screen. It's like you're there. Space is all around you."

One current program lets you zoom through the Valles Marineris, one of the longest canyons on Mars. This wild ride is based on real photos taken by *Viking* spacecraft. Also, NASA scientists hope that, one day, astronauts will see a planet's surface through the eyes of a roving robot. They will use goggles and data gloves to command the robot from the safety of a space ship or home base.

Virtual reality may sound like a thing of the future, but some kids are already experiencing a version of it. The Power Glove is similar to expensive data gloves. With the Power Glove, you don't actually enter the video game world. But it does let you move things around the screen by pointing instead of using a joystick.

And recently, Meredith Bricken, a scientist at the University of Washington, taught kids at local schools how to program their own virtual worlds. She gave the kids software that allowed them to create 3-D drawings on the computer. Some of their projects included a pool you could dive into, a space station on the moon and a mountain that could be explored from the inside out.

"Virtual reality brings out your sense of adventure," Bricken says. "Adults have mapped the real world pretty thoroughly. But now there are new worlds to explore."

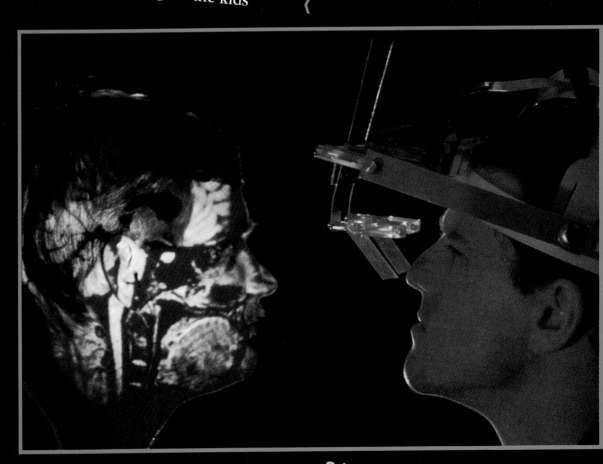

Scientists at the University of North Carolina peer into a virtual head. They hope to someday treat sick patients this way.

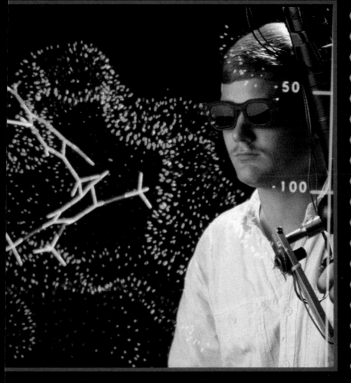

By "pushing" one virtual molecule against another, scientists can see how different chemicals react to each other.

LESSON 3 REVIEW

The technology that allows the development of virtual reality has been used to build games and museum exhibits. What other uses can virtual reality programs have? How could virtual reality help you to learn science?

 DOUBLE CHECK

SECTION D REVIEW

1. How would your life be different if electric current had not been discovered?

2. How has the invention of binary code changed communications?

3. List two ways computers could be used in the future. Explain how these uses would change your life.

I REFLECT

It's time to think about the ideas you have discovered during your investigations. Think, too, about your many accomplishments.

SUMMARIZE

Answer the following in your Science Log.

1. What **I Wonder** questions have you answered in your investigations? What new questions have you asked?

2. What have you discovered about electricity, light, and sound? How have your ideas changed?

3. Did any of your discoveries surprise you? Explain.

Series Circuit

In a series circuit, the electricity has to go through each object in the circuit. If one object doesn't work, electricity won't go through any part of the circuit.

▲ Earmuffs keep your ears warm, but they can also make it more difficult to hear sounds.

▲ Some types of ear coverings are used to protect a person's ears from harmful loud noises.

CONNECT IDEAS

1. Think about what would have happened if you had tried using a rubber band instead of a paper clip when you built your switch. Why do you think wires usually are covered with rubber?

2. Rainbows are formed because sunlight splits into colors. Explain how you think a rainbow is formed in the sky. Why do rainbows appear after a rainstorm?

3. How do you think programs are transmitted to your television set? Write a paragraph using what you've learned about telephones and fax machines.

4. Why does covering your ears make it more difficult to hear sounds around you?

SCIENCE PORTFOLIO

1. Complete your Science Experiences Record.

2. Choose a few samples of your best work from each section to include in your Science Portfolio.

3. On A Guide to My Science Portfolio, tell why you chose each sample.

I SHARE

Scientists share their discoveries and ideas and learn from one another. How can you share what you've learned?

Decide

► what you want to say.

► what the best way is to get your message across.

Share

► what you did and why.

► what worked and what didn't work.

► what conclusions you have drawn.

► what else you'd like to find out.

Find Out

► what classmates like about what you shared—and why.

► what questions your classmates have.

Connect these items to make a parallel circuit.

I ACT

Science is more than discoveries—it is also what you do with your discoveries. How might you use what you have learned about electricity, light, sound, and communication?

▶ Invent a flashlight that can send its beam around a corner. Demonstrate it for your class.

▶ Set up a musical instrument demonstration in your classroom to show how different sounds are produced.

▶ Draw a poster that compares parallel and series circuits, and use it to explain the difference to your family.

▶ Make a display that shows how communication has improved from the time of the Pony Express until today. Put the display someplace in your school where other classes can view it.

▶ Write a short play about the invention of the telegraph. Put on the play for other classes.

THE LANGUAGE OF SCIENCE

The language of science helps people communicate clearly. Here are some vocabulary words you can use when you talk about electricity, light, sound, and communication with friends, family, and others.

binary code—a code used in computers and other electronic communication devices. This code has only two signals, which are produced by switching electric current on or off. Many combinations of *on* or *off* signals are used for letters, pictures, and numbers. **(C72)**

circuit—a path that electricity follows from one point to another. Series circuits and parallel circuits are two kinds of circuits. **(C20)**

compute—to do mathematical calculations. **(C72)**

current electricity—a type of electricity in which the electric charges are in motion and can be made to flow through wires or other conductors. **(C20)**

▲ Electricity is transmitted through wires.

electric charges—these are a part of every object, but they are too small to be seen. Charges are either positive or negative. Negative charges can be rubbed off one object and built up on another object. When an object has more positive charges than negative charges, it is positively charged. When an object has more negative charges than positive charges, it is negatively charged. **(C14)**

▲ Static electricity

electromagnet—a type of magnet that requires electricity in order to work. If the electricity is shut off, the magnet will not function. These magnets can be very powerful. Their power is increased by increasing the amount of electricity flowing through them or the number of turns of wire in their coils. **(C29)**

▲ Electromagnet

ENIAC—stands for *Electronic Numerical Integrator and Computer.* It was the first computer and only processed numbers, but it worked very rapidly. **(C66)**

fax machine—short for *facsimile machine.* Translates print or pictures into binary code. The code is sent over telephone wires to another fax machine, which translates the code back into print or a picture. **(C78)**

Morse code—Samuel Morse was credited with the invention of the telegraph. He developed a code of dots and dashes that matched the letters of the alphabet. Telegraph operators could send messages over wires using the code. **(C26)**

opaque materials—materials that do not allow any light to pass through them. Opaque materials cause shadows to form. Examples include solid objects such as a brick, a piece of cardboard, or a building. **(C41)**

parallel circuit—an electric circuit that has more than one path for the electric current to flow through. This means that if one item connected to the circuit goes out, the other items in the circuit will continue to receive current, so they will continue to work. **(C24)**

▲ Parallel circuit

prism—a triangular piece of glass or plastic. When white light passes through a prism, its waves are bent and spread apart into different colors. Water droplets can act as prisms. That is the way a rainbow forms. **(C38)**

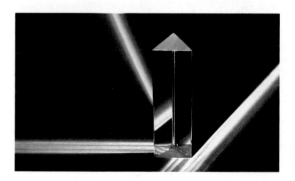

reflect—to bounce back. Mirrors reflect light, and satellites can reflect radio waves and microwaves. **(C37)**

series circuit—an electric circuit that has only one path for the electric current to flow through. The current must flow through each item before passing to the next. This means that if one item connected to the circuit goes out, the other items in the circuit will not continue to receive current, so they will not continue to work. **(C24)**

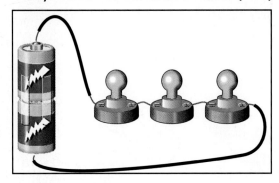

▲ Series circuit

silicon—a chemical found in sand that is important because electricity can travel through it. Used in microchips, it has allowed the development of smaller computers such as the laptop and those that can be put into watches. **(C70)**

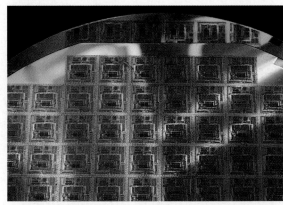

▲ Silicon chips on a wafer

sound waves—back and forth movements in solids, liquids, or gases caused by vibrations. Sound waves are interpreted by the brain. **(C50)**

switch—an object that is used to complete or interrupt a circuit through which electricity flows. A switch must be made of a material through which electricity can flow, such as metal. **(C21)**

telegraph—a device that uses electricity to send messages. By switching electric current on and off, a series of "dots" and "dashes" could be sent across electric wires to distant places. These dots and dashes made up a code, called Morse code, which stand for the letters of the alphabet. **(C25)**

translucent materials—materials that allow some but not all light to pass through them. Examples include frosted glass and some thin fabrics. **(C41)**

transparent materials—materials that allow almost all light to pass through them. Examples include clear glass and clear plastic. **(C41)**

virtual reality—recent computer development that allows game players to feel as if they are inside the game. It is also being developed for use by doctors, air traffic controllers, scientists, and salespeople. **(C82)**

REFERENCE HANDBOOK

Safety in the Classroom

Doing activities in science can be fun, but you need to be sure you do them safely. It is up to you, your teacher, and your classmates to make your classroom a safe place for science activities.

Think about what causes most accidents in everyday life—being careless, not paying attention, and showing off. The same kinds of behavior cause accidents in the science classroom.

Here are some ways to make your classroom a safe place.

THINK AHEAD.

Study the steps of the activity so you know what to expect. If you have any questions about the steps, ask your teacher to explain. Be sure you understand any safety symbols that are shown in the activity.

WATCH YOUR EYES.

Wear safety goggles anytime you are directed to do so. If you should ever get any substance in your eyes, tell your teacher right away.

BE NEAT.

Keep your work area clean. If you have long hair, pull it back so it doesn't get in the way. If you have long sleeves, roll them or push them up to keep them away from your experiment.

YUCK!

Never eat or drink anything during a science activity unless you are told to do so by your teacher.

OOPS!

If you should have an accident that causes a spill or breaks something, or if you get cut, tell your teacher right away.

KEEP IT CLEAN.

Always clean up when you have finished your activity. Put everything away and wipe your work area. Last of all, wash your hands.

DON'T GET SHOCKED.

Sometimes you need to use electric appliances, such as lamps, in an activity. You always need to be careful around electricity. Be sure that electric cords are in a safe place where you can't trip over them. Don't ever pull a plug out of an outlet by pulling on the cord.

REFERENCE HANDBOOK

Safety in the Classroom

Doing activities in science can be fun, but you need to be sure you do them safely. It is up to you, your teacher, and your classmates to make your classroom a safe place for science activities.

Think about what causes most accidents in everyday life—being careless, not paying attention, and showing off. The same kinds of behavior cause accidents in the science classroom.

Here are some ways to make your classroom a safe place.

WATCH YOUR EYES.

Wear safety goggles anytime you are directed to do so. If you should ever get any substance in your eyes, tell your teacher right away.

THINK AHEAD.

Study the steps of the activity so you know what to expect. If you have any questions about the steps, ask your teacher to explain. Be sure you understand any safety symbols that are shown in the activity.

BE NEAT.

Keep your work area clean. If you have long hair, pull it back so it doesn't get in the way. If you have long sleeves, roll them or push them up to keep them away from your experiment.

YUCK!

Never eat or drink anything during a science activity unless you are told to do so by your teacher.

OOPS!

If you should have an accident that causes a spill or breaks something, or if you get cut, tell your teacher right away.

KEEP IT CLEAN.

Always clean up when you have finished your activity. Put everything away and wipe your work area. Last of all, wash your hands.

DON'T GET SHOCKED.

Sometimes you need to use electric appliances, such as lamps, in an activity. You always need to be careful around electricity. Be sure that electric cords are in a safe place where you can't trip over them. Don't ever pull a plug out of an outlet by pulling on the cord.

Safety Symbols

In some activities, you will see a symbol that stands for what you need to do to stay safe. Do what the symbol stands for.

 This is a general symbol that tells you to be careful. Reading the steps of the activity will tell you exactly what you need to do to be safe.

 You will need to protect your eyes if you see this symbol. Put on safety goggles and leave them on for the entire activity.

 This symbol tells you that you will be using something sharp in the activity. Be careful not to cut or poke yourself or others.

 This symbol tells you something hot will be used in the activity. Be careful not to get burned or to cause someone else to get burned.

 This symbol tells you to put on an apron to protect your clothing.

 Don't touch! This symbol tells you that you will need to touch something that is hot. Use a thermal mitt to protect your hand.

 This symbol tells you that you will be using electric equipment. Use proper safety procedures.

Using a Hand Lens

A hand lens magnifies objects, or makes them look larger than they are.

▲ This object is not in focus.

Sometimes objects are too small for you to see easily without some help. You might want to see details that you cannot see with your eyes alone. When this happens, you can use a hand lens.

To use a hand lens, first place the object you want to look at on a flat surface, such as a table. Next, hold the hand lens over the object. At first, the object may appear blurry, like the object in **A**. Move the hand lens toward or away from the object until the object comes into sharp focus, as shown in **B**.

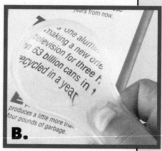

▲ This object is focused clearly.

Making a Water-Drop Lens

There may be times when you want to use a hand lens but there isn't one around. If that happens, you can make a water-drop lens to help you in the same way a hand lens does. A water-drop lens is best used to make flat objects, such as pieces of paper and leaves, seem larger.

MATERIALS
- sheet of acetate
- 2 rectangular rubber erasers
- water
- dropper

DO THIS

❶ Place the object to be magnified on a table between two identical erasers.

❷ Place a sheet of acetate on top of the erasers so that the sheet of acetate is about 1 cm above the object.

❸ Use the dropper to place one drop of water on the surface of the sheet over the object. Don't make the drop too large or it will make things look bent.

A water-drop lens can magnify objects. ▶

Caring For and Using a Microscope

A microscope, like a hand lens, magnifies objects. However, a microscope can increase the detail you see by increasing the number of times an object is magnified.

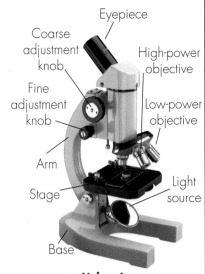

▲ **Light microscope**

CARING FOR A MICROSCOPE

- Always use two hands when you carry a microscope.
- Never touch any of the lenses of the microscope with your fingers.

USING A MICROSCOPE

1 Raise the eyepiece as far as you can using the coarse-adjustment knob. Place the slide you wish to view on the stage.

2 Always start by using the lowest power. The lowest-power lens is usually the shortest. Start with the lens in the lowest position it can go without touching the slide.

3 Look through the eyepiece and begin adjusting the eyepiece upward with the coarse-adjustment knob. When the slide is close to being in focus, use the fine-adjustment knob.

4 When you want to use the higher-power lens, first focus the slide under low power. Then, watching carefully to make sure that the lens will not hit the slide, turn the higher-power lens into place. Use only the fine-adjustment knob when looking through the higher-power lens.

Some of you may use a Brock microscope. This is a sturdy microscope that has only one lens.

1 Place the object to be viewed on the stage. Move the long tube, containing the lens, close to the stage.

2 Put your eye on the eyepiece, and begin raising the tube until the object comes into focus.

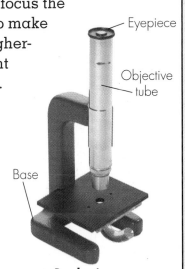

▲ **Brock microscope**

Using a Dropper

Use a dropper when you need to add small amounts of a liquid to another material.

A dropper has two main parts. One is a large empty part called a *bulb*. You hold the bulb and squeeze it to use the dropper. The other part of a dropper is long and narrow and is called a *tube*.

DO THIS

1️⃣ Use a clean dropper for each liquid you measure.

2️⃣ With the dropper out of the liquid, squeeze the bulb and keep it squeezed. Then dip the end of the tube into the liquid.

3️⃣ Release the pressure on the bulb. As you do so, you will see the liquid enter the tube.

▲ Using a dropper correctly

4️⃣ Take the dropper from the liquid, and move it to the place you want to put the liquid. If you are putting the liquid into another liquid, do not let the dropper touch the surface of the second liquid.

5️⃣ Gently squeeze the bulb until one drop comes out of the tube. Repeat slowly until you have measured out the right number of drops.

▲ Using a dropper incorrectly

Measuring Liquids

Use a beaker, a measuring cup, or a graduated cylinder to measure liquids accurately.

Containers for measuring liquids are made of clear or translucent materials so that you can see the liquid inside them. On the outside of each of these measuring tools, you will see lines and numbers that make up a scale. On most of the containers used by scientists, the scale is in milliliters (mL).

DO THIS

1 Pour the liquid you want to measure into one of the measuring containers. Make sure your measuring container is on a flat, stable surface, with the measuring scale facing you.

2 Look at the liquid through the container. Move so that your eyes are even with the surface of the liquid in the container.

3 To read the volume of the liquid, find the scale line that is even with the top of the liquid. In narrow containers, the surface of the liquid may look curved. Take your reading at the lowest point of the curve.

▲ There are 32 mL of liquid in this graduated cylinder.

4 Sometimes the surface of the liquid may not be exactly even with a line. In that case, you will need to estimate the volume of the liquid. Decide which line the liquid is closer to, and use that number.

▲ There are 27 mL of liquid in this beaker.

Using a Thermometer

Determine temperature readings of the air and most liquids by using a thermometer with a standard scale.

Most thermometers are thin tubes of glass that are filled with a red or silver liquid. As the temperature goes up, the liquid in the tube rises. As the temperature goes down, the liquid sinks. The tube is marked with lines and numbers that provide a temperature scale in degrees. Scientists use the Celsius scale to measure temperature. A temperature reading of 27 degrees Celsius is written 27°C.

DO THIS

1 Place the thermometer in the liquid whose temperature you want to record, but don't rest the bulb of the thermometer on the bottom or side of the container. If you are measuring the temperature of the air, make sure that the thermometer is not in direct sunlight or in line with a direct light source.

2 Move so that your eyes are even with the liquid in the thermometer.

3 If you are measuring a material that is not being heated or cooled, wait about two minutes for the reading to become stable. Find the scale line that meets the top of the liquid in the thermometer, and read the temperature.

4 If the material you are measuring is being heated or cooled, you will not be able to wait before taking your measurements. Measure as quickly as you can.

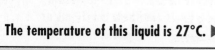

The temperature of this liquid is 27°C. ▶

Making a Thermometer

If you don't have a thermometer, you can make a simple one easily. The simple thermometer won't give you an exact temperature reading, but you can use it to tell if the temperature is going up or going down.

MATERIALS
- small, narrow-mouthed jar
- colored water
- clear plastic straw
- ruler
- clay
- dropper
- pen, pencil, or marker
- bowl of ice
- bowl of warm water

DO THIS

1 Add colored water to the jar until it is nearly full.

2 Place the straw in the jar. Finish filling the jar with water, but leave about 1 cm of space at the top.

3 Lift the straw until 10 cm of it sticks up out of the jar. Use the clay to seal the mouth of the jar.

4 Use the dropper to add colored water to the straw until the straw is at least half full.

5 On the straw, mark the level of the water. "S" stands for *start*.

6 To get an idea of how your thermometer works, place the jar in a bowl of ice. Wait several minutes, and then mark the new water level on the straw. This new water level should be marked C for *cold*.

7 Take the jar out of the bowl of ice, and let it return to room temperature. Next, place the jar in a bowl of warm water. Wait several minutes, and then mark the new water level on the straw. This level can be labeled W for *warm*.

—W

—S

—C

▶ You can use a thermometer like this to decide if the temperature of a liquid or the air is going up or down.

Using a Balance

Use a balance to measure an object's mass. Mass is the amount of matter an object has.

Most balances look like the one shown. They have two pans. In one pan, you place the object you want to measure. In the other pan, you place standard masses. Standard masses are objects that have a known mass. Grams are the units used to measure mass for most scientific activities.

DO THIS

1 First, make certain the empty pans are balanced. They are in balance if the pointer is at the middle mark on the base. If the pointer is not at this mark, move the slider to the right or left. Your teacher will help if you cannot balance the pans.

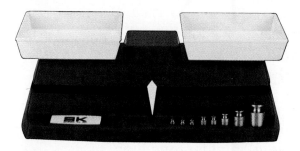

◀ **These pans are balanced and ready to be used to find the mass of an object.**

2 Place the object you wish to measure in one pan. The pointer will move toward the pan without the object in it.

3 Add the standard masses to the other pan. As you add masses, you should see the pointer begin to move. When the pointer is at the middle mark again, the pans are balanced.

4 Add the numbers on the masses you used. The total is the mass of the object you measured.

These pans are unbalanced. ▶

Making a Balance

If you do not have a balance, you can make one. A balance requires only a few simple materials. You can use nonstandard masses such as paper clips or nickels. This type of balance is best for measuring small masses.

DO THIS

1 If the ruler has holes in it, tie the string through the center hole. If it does not have holes, tie the string around the middle of the ruler.

2 Tape the other end of the string to a table. Allow the ruler to hang down from the side of the table. Adjust the ruler so that it is level.

3 Unbend the end of each paper clip slightly. Push these ends through the paper cups as shown. Attach each cup to the ruler by using the paper clips.

4 Adjust the cups until the ruler is level again.

MATERIALS
- 1 sturdy plastic or wooden ruler
- string
- transparent tape
- 2 paper cups
- 2 large paper clips

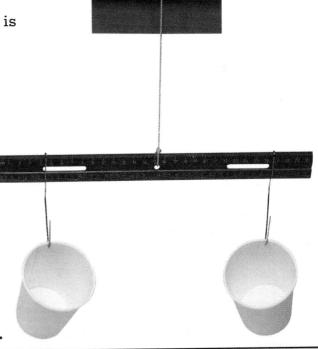

▶ **This balance is ready for use.**

Using a Spring Scale

A spring scale is a tool you use to measure the force of gravity on objects. You find the weight of the objects and use newtons as the unit of measurement for the force of gravity. You also use the spring scale and newtons to measure other forces.

A spring scale has two main parts. One part is a spring with a hook on the end. The hook is used to connect an object to the spring scale. The other part is a scale with numbers that tell you how many newtons of force are acting on the object.

DO THIS

With an Object at Rest

1 With the object resting on the table, hook the spring scale to it. Do not stretch the spring at this point.

2 Lift the scale and object with a smooth motion. Do not jerk them upward.

3 Wait until any motion in the spring comes to a stop. Then read the number of newtons from the scale.

With an Object in Motion

1 With the object resting on the table, hook the spring scale to it. Do not stretch the spring.

2 Pull the object smoothly across the table. Do not jerk the object. If you pull with a jerky motion, the spring scale will wiggle too much for you to get a good reading.

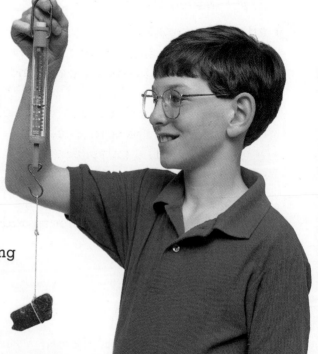

3 As you are pulling, read the number of newtons you are using to pull the object.

Making a Spring Scale

If you do not have a spring scale, you can make one by following the directions below.

DO THIS

1 Staple one end of the rubber band (the part with the sharp curve) to the middle of one end of the cardboard so that the rubber band hangs down the length of the cardboard. Color the loose end of the rubber band with a marker to make it easy to see.

2 Bend the paper clip so that it is slightly open and forms a hook. Hang the paper clip by its unopened end from the rubber band.

3 Put the narrow paper strip across the rubber band, and staple the strip to the cardboard. The rubber band and hook must be able to move easily.

4 While holding the cardboard upright, hang one 100-g mass from the hook. Allow the mass to come to rest, and mark the position of the bottom of the rubber band on the cardboard. Label this position on the cardboard 1 N. Add another 100-g mass for a total of 200 g.

5 Continue to add masses and mark the cardboard. Each 100-g mass adds a force of about 1 N.

MATERIALS
- heavy cardboard (10cm x 30cm)
- large rubber band
- stapler
- marker
- large paper clip
- paper strip (about 1 cm x 3 cm)
- 100-g masses (about 1 N each)

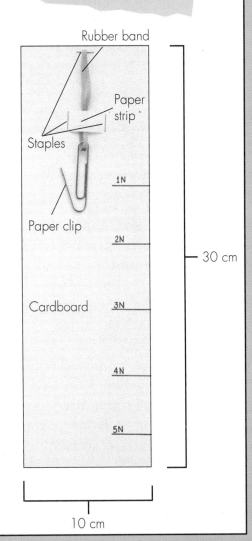

Rubber band

Paper strip

Staples

Paper clip

Cardboard

1N
2N
3N
4N
5N

30 cm

10 cm

Working Like a Scientist
Is Soup a Lowfat Food?

Mrs. Hazlet's fourth-grade class had learned about nutrition. They knew what they should eat and what they shouldn't. Fat was one of the things that they knew was not good for them in large amounts. Mrs. Hazlet had told them that they should not have more than about 75 grams of fat per day. She had the class form groups to find one kind of food that is low in fat. Margie, Anna, and Kevin were all in one group.

Anna said, "Where do we start?"

Margie said, "Let's start with soup. Soup shouldn't have much fat. It's mostly water."

Kevin said, "That sounds right. Maybe soup would be a good food to start with."

"Okay," Anna said. "What kind of soup? Do all soups have the same amount of fat?"

"That's a good question. I don't know the answer," Kevin said. "Do you?"

"No," Margie said.

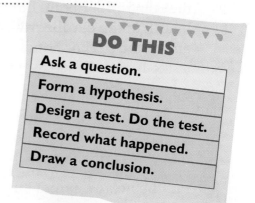

DO THIS
Ask a question.
Form a hypothesis.
Design a test. Do the test.
Record what happened.
Draw a conclusion.

Asking a question is the first part of any investigation. You must ask your question carefully so that you will be able to test it. Anna asked, "Do all soups have the same amount of fat?" That question can be answered scientifically. She did not ask, "Are all soups the same?" That question would be hard to answer scientifically.

The next step of any investigation is to think of one answer to your question. This possible answer to your question is called a hypothesis. When you think of the answer, you are *forming a hypothesis.* The question Anna asked was, "Do all soups have the same amount of fat?" There are just two possible answers to that question—yes or no. Read on to find out what Margie, Anna, and Kevin thought.

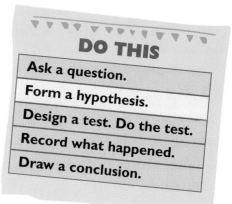

DO THIS

| Ask a question. |
| Form a hypothesis. |
| Design a test. Do the test. |
| Record what happened. |
| Draw a conclusion. |

Anna said, "I think that soups may have different amounts of fat. Some soups may have more and some may have less."

Kevin said, "Why do you think that?"

Anna said, "Some soups are like water. Some soups are more like milk and cream. Clam chowder is like milk."

Margie said, "*One* kind is. I've also had a kind that's like tomato soup, so it's more like water. But Anna may be right. I think I agree with her."

Kevin shrugged his shoulders. "Her idea sounds okay to me. But let's make sure we're all thinking the same thing. We think soups have different amounts of fat. Soups that are like water may have less fat. Soups that are more like milk may have more fat."

"Right," Anna said. "So how do we find out?"

"We investigate!" Kevin said.

After you ask a question and form a hypothesis, you must think of a way to test your answer. You must *design an experiment* to test whether your answer is correct.

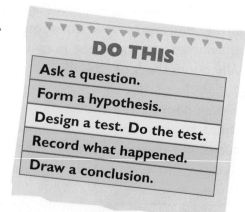

DO THIS

Ask a question.

Form a hypothesis.

Design a test. Do the test.

Record what happened.

Draw a conclusion.

Margie said, "This should be easy to test. We can get the labels from a lot of different soup cans."

"Right," Anna said. "We'll get the labels and classify the soups into two groups, creamy soups and watery soups."

Kevin said, "Then we can read the labels and find out how much fat each kind of soup has."

"Yes, but we need to be sure to use the same amount of soup for each measurement," Anna said.

"The labels will tell us the size of one serving. We can just compare the ones that are the same," said Kevin.

"We need to get labels from a lot of different kinds of soups. And we need to know if the soups are creamy or watery," Margie said.

"That's easy," Anna said. "We'll ask the other people in the class to bring in soup labels and describe each soup to us so that we can classify it."

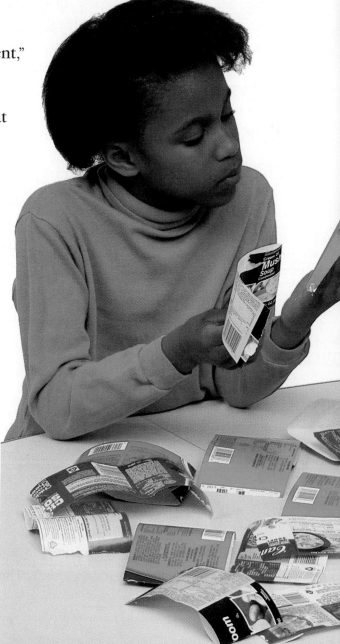

Nutrition Facts Serv. Size 1 cup (240mL) condensed soup Servings About 1 **Calories** 140 Fat Cal. 50 *Percent Daily Values (DV) are based on a 2,000-calorie diet.	Amount/serving	%DV*	Amount/serving	%DV*
	Total Fat 5g	4%	**Total Carb.** 18g	3%
	Sat. Fat 2g	5%	Fiber 0g	0%
	Cholest. Less Than 10mg	1%	Sugars 0g	
	Sodium 1660mg	35%	**Protein** 6g	
	Vitamin A 35% • Vitamin C 0% • Calcium 0% • Iron 2%			

Margie, Anna, and Kevin designed a way to test their hypothesis. They also planned a way to collect the information. Another word for information is *data*. The next important step in their investigation was to find a way to *record the data*.

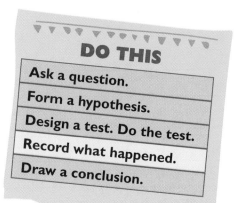

▼ ▼ ▼ ▼ ▼ ▼ ▼ ▼ ▼ ▼ ▼ ▼ ▼

DO THIS

Ask a question.

Form a hypothesis.

Design a test. Do the test.

Record what happened.

Draw a conclusion.

Kevin, Margie, and Anna sat at a table with what seemed like hundreds of soup-can labels in front of them.

"Oh, no," Anna said. "What are we going to do? How can we make any sense out of all of this?"

Margie frowned. "It's really a mess. But what if we started by just separating the labels into groups? Then we could make a chart. We could label one column *Creamy Soups* and one *Watery Soups* and list the grams of fat in a serving of each kind of soup. Most of the labels list an eight-ounce serving, so we could use those and throw the rest away."

Kevin said, "Good idea. We could list each kind of soup and the number of grams of fat it has in the right column."

"Oh, I see," Anna said. "Then we can add up the total grams of fat in the soups when we get done with our test."

Margie agreed. But then she thought about something else. "There's one more thing we have to remember. We must have exactly the same number of creamy soups and watery soups. If we don't, it would not be a fair test."

● ● ● ● ● ● ● ● ● ● ●

Kevin, Anna, and Margie sorted their labels. You can see part of their data in this chart.

Data from Soup Labels		
Names of Soups	Fat in Creamy Soups/ Per 8 Ounces	Fat in Watery Soups/ Per 8 Ounces
Cream of Potato	3g	
Cream of Broccoli	5g	
Cream of Mushroom	7g	
Chicken Noodle		3g
Bean with Bacon		4g
Beef Noodle		4g

"But this chart is hard to read," Margie said.

"I know," Anna said. "Let's make a bar graph. We can have two bars to show the grams of fat in watery and creamy soups."

Kevin drew the bar graph you see here.

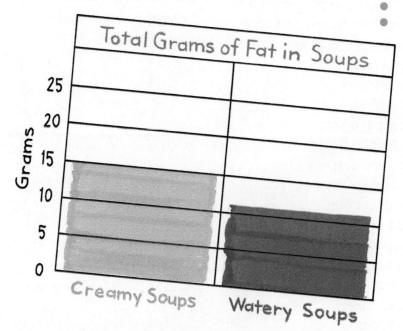

After you have collected the data, you need to see what it tells you about whether your answer to the question was correct or incorrect. You do this by seeing if the data supports your hypothesis and by *drawing a conclusion.*

DO THIS

| Ask a question. |
| Form a hypothesis. |
| Design a test. Do the test. |
| Record what happened. |
| Draw a conclusion. |

"Well," Anna said, "what do you think?"

"I don't know," Kevin said. "It seems to me that creamy soups and watery soups can have the same amount of fat."

"That's what it looks like to me," Margie said. "Look here," she said as she pointed to the bar graph. "These are nearly equal."

"They are," Anna said. "Are you surprised? I am."

"I am, too," Margie said. "Water doesn't have any fat, but some watery soups sure do."

"I think we've found out something important that we can share with the class," Kevin said. "Maybe a lot of people think the way we did!"

"You're right," Anna said. "Let's make a poster to show everyone what we found out."

If your first answer is not correct, you have not failed. Margie, Anna, and Kevin learned something surprising about soups. The data they collected didn't support their hypothesis that watery soups would have less fat than creamy soups. This often occurs with an investigation. When something happens that you don't expect, you can learn from it. You can use that information to start asking other questions. You may need to form a different hypothesis and design a new experiment. However, you are able to build on what you know.

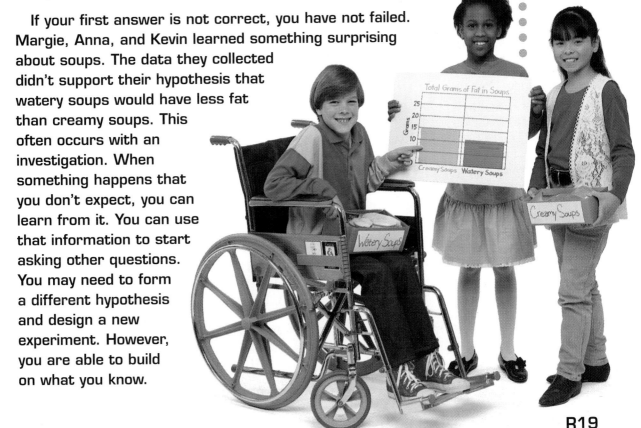

R19

INDEX

Note: Page numbers in italics indicate illustrations.

ACKNOWLEDGMENTS

For permission to reprint copyrighted material, grateful acknowledgment is made to the following sources:

Addison-Wesley Publishing Company, Inc.: From "Potatoes from the Andes to You" in *The Amazing Potato Book* by Paulette Bourgeois. Text © 1991 by Paulette Bourgeois.

Atheneum Publishers, an imprint of Macmillan Publishing Company: "Fossils" from *Something New Begins* by Lilian Moore. Text copyright © 1982 by Lilian Moore.

Children's Television Workshop, New York, NY: "Virtual Reality: Computers Create Lifelike Worlds You Can Step Into" by Brianna Politzer from *3-2-1 Contact* Magazine, May 1992. Text copyright 1992 by Children's Television Workshop.

Cobblehill Books, a division of Penguin Books USA Inc.: Cover photograph from *Sea Otter Rescue* by Roland Smith. Copyright © 1990 by Roland Smith.

Harcourt Brace & Company: Cover illustration from *The Great Kapok Tree* by Lynne Cherry. Copyright © 1990 by Lynne Cherry.

Highlights for Children, Inc., Columbus, OH: "The Peanut Patch" by Eileen Van Kirk from *Highlights for Children* Magazine, June 1992. Text copyright © 1992 by Highlights for Children, Inc.

Lerner Publications Company, Minneapolis, MN: From *The Great Barrier Reef: A Living Laboratory* (Retitled: "An Australian Mangrove Forest") by Rebecca L. Johnson. Text copyright © 1991 by Lerner Publications Company.

Little, Brown and Company: From "The Rainbow" in *One at a Time* by David McCord. Text copyright 1935 by David McCord.

Lothrop, Lee & Shepard Books, a division of William Morrow & Company, Inc.: Cover photograph from *Earth Alive!* by Sandra Markle. Photograph copyright © 1991 by Galen Rowell/Mountain Light Photography.

Macmillan Publishing Company, a Division of Macmillan, Inc.: Cover photograph by George Ancona from *Mom Can't See Me* by Sally Hobart Alexander. Photograph copyright © 1990 by George Ancona. Cover illustration by Jennifer Eachus from *In the Middle of the Night* by Kathy Henderson. Illustration copyright © 1992 by Jennifer Eachus. Cover illustration from *The Rock* by Peter Parnall. Copyright © 1991 by Peter Parnall.

Margaret K. McElderry Books, an imprint of Macmillan Publishing Company: Cover illustration by Ian Wallace from *The Name of the Tree* by Celia Barker Lottridge. Illustration copyright © 1989 by Ian Wallace.

National Geographic WORLD: From "Glaciers: Rivers of Ice" (Retitled: "Huge Rivers of Ice") in *National Geographic WORLD* Magazine, January 1990. Text copyright 1990 by National Geographic Society. Illustrations by Jaime Quintero and George Constantino. From "Leafing Leopards! Why Am I Green?" in *National Geographic WORLD* Magazine, June 1992. Text copyright 1992 by National Geographic Society.

Orchard Books, New York: Cover illustration from *The Life and Times of the Apple* by Charles Micucci. Copyright © 1992 by Charles Micucci.

Clarkson N. Potter, Inc., a member of the Crown Publishing Group: From *Our Changing World: The Forest* by David Bellamy. Text copyright © 1988 by Botanical Enterprises Publications Ltd.

G. P. Putnam's Sons: Cover illustration by David Shannon from *The Boy Who Lived with the Seals* by Rafe Martin. Illustration copyright © 1993 by David Shannon.

San Juan School District, Montezuma Creek Elementary School, Montezuma Creek, UT: "Canyons" by Andrew Jones from *Rising Voices,* selected by Arlene B. Hirschfelder and Beverly R. Singer. Published by Charles Scribner's Sons, an imprint of Macmillan Publishing Company.

Simon & Schuster Books for Young Readers, New York: Cover illustration from *A Tree in a Forest* by Jan Thornhill. © 1991 by Jan Thornhill.

Gareth Stevens Publishing, Milwaukee, WI: "Rainforest Medicines" from *Why Are the Rainforests Vanishing?* by Isaac Asimov. Text © 1992 by Nightfall, Inc. and Martin H. Greenberg.

Franklin Watts, Inc., New York: From *Spill! The Story of the Exxon Valdez* by Terry Carr. Text copyright © 1991 by Terry Carr. Map courtesy of Vantage Art, Inc.

PHOTO CREDITS:

To The Student: Page: iv Dennis Galante/Envision; v(t), NASA; v(b), Francois Gohier/Photo Researchers; vi(l), The Bettmann Archive; vi(r), Westlight; vii(l), Tom Till; vii(r), Sinclair Stammers/Photo Researchers; viii(l), Phil Degginger/Color Pic; viii(r), E.R. Degginger/Color Pic; x, The Stock Market; xi(t), Comstock; xi(b), Myrleen Ferguson/PhotoEdit; xii, Comstock; xiii, David Young-Wolff/PhotoEdit; xiv(l), Comstock; xiv(r), David Young-Wolff/PhotoEdit; xv(t), Richard Nowitz/Photo Researchers; xv(b), Annette Stahl; xvi(l), David Young-Wolff/PhotoEdit; xvi(r), Michael Newman/PhotoEdit.

Unit A: Harcourt Brace & Company Photographs: A4-A5, A6(t), A6 (b), A8, A9, A10-A11, A18, A21, A24, A25, A29, A36, A41(t), A41(b), A42(t), A42 (b), A43(t), A43(b), A49 (b), A50, A58, A66, A70(b), A74, A80(t), A80 (bl), A80(br), A81, A82 (r), A89(b), A92(t), A92(b), A93(t).

All Other Photographs: Unit A Divider: Manfred Gottschalk/Tom Stack & Assoc. A1, Manfred Gottschalk/Tom Stack & Assoc.; A2-A3 (bg), Willard Clay/FPG International; A3 (inset) William E. Ferguson; A7, Erick L. Heyer/Grant Heilman; A12 (bg), Obremski/The Image Bank; A12 (t), John Colwell/Grant Heilman; A12, (inset) Dennis Galante/Envision; A27 (t), Gerhard Gscheidle/Peter Arnold, Inc.; A27(b), MacDonald/Envision; A28, Grant Heilman; A32 (t), Manfred Gottschalk/Tom Stack & Associates; A32 (b), Marc & EvelyneBernheim/Woodfin Camp & Associates; A33 (l), Jean Higgins/Envision; A33 (t), Peter Menzel/Stock, Boston; A33 (b), M. Zur/Envision; A37 (l), Steven Mark/Envision; A37 (r), Rudy Muller/Envision; A38, (t), Guy Powers/Envision; A38 (c), Amy Reichman/Envision; A38 (b), Dennis Gallante/Envision; A39, Steven Mark Needham/Envision; A40 (t), Alan Pitcairn/Grant Heilman ; A40 (inset) Amy Reichman/Envision; A44 (l), Grant Heilman/Grant Heilman A44 (r), Grant Heilman/Grant Heilman ,A45 (t), Larry Lefever/Grant Heilman ; A45 (c), Thomas Kitchin/Tom Stack & Associates; A45 (bl), Tim Gibson/Envision; A45 (br), Grant Heilman/Grant Heilman ;A46 (t), Grant Heilman/Grant Heilman ;A46 (b), Grant Heilman ;A46 (tl), Robert Barclay/Grant Heilman ;A46 (br), Grant Heilman/Grant Heilman ; A47 (l), Don & Pat Valenti/Tom Stack & Associates;

A47 (r), Grant Heilman;A48 (t), Grant Heilman/Grant Heilman;A48, (b), Grant Heilman/Grant Heilman ;A49 (t), Wanda LaRock/Envision; A49 (c), Barry L. Runk/Grant Heilman ; A52-A53 (t), Timothy O'Keefe/Bruce Coleman Inc.; A55 (l), Barry L. Runk/Grant Heilman;A55 (r), Runk/Schoenberger/Grant Heilman ;A55 (c), Runk/Schoenberger/Grant Heilman ; A55 (inset) Roger & Joy Spurr/Bruce Coleman Inc.; A64 (bg), Comstock; A64 (t), Michael Ventura/Bruce Coleman Inc.; A64 (inset) E. R. Degginger/Color-Pic; A65 (l), Runk Schoenberger/Grant Heilman; A65 (r), Runk Schoenberger/Grant Heilman; A67(t), Grant Heilman/Grant Heilman ;A67 (c), Grant Heilman/Grant Heilman ; A67 (b), S.L. Craig Jr./Bruce Coleman; A68 (c), Amy Etra/Photo Edit; A68 (b), Amy Etra/Photo Edit; A68-A69 (t), Amy Etra/Photo Edit; A6 (t), The Image Bank; A69(b), Amy Etra/Photo Edit; A7(l), Amy Etra/PhotoEdit; A70(r), Amy Etra/Photo Edit; A7 (c), Viesti Associates, Inc.; A71, Roger Wilmhurst/Bruce Coleman, Inc.; A73(r), Keith Gunnar/Bruce Coleman Inc.; A73 (c), Wendell Metzen/Bruce Coleman Inc.; A75, Ana M. Venegas; A7 (b), Ana M. Venegas; A76-A77 (t), Ana M. Venegas; A78-A79 (t), Lisa Quinones//Black Star; A79(b), Lisa Quinones/Black Star; A82 (bg),Gary Cralle/The Image Bank; A82, (inset), James H. Carmichael/Bruce Coleman Inc.; A84 (t), George H. Harrison/Bruce Coleman; A84 (c), Martin Rogers/Woodfin Camp & Associates; A84 (b), Kevin Schafer/Peter Arnold, Inc.; A85(tl), Grant Heilman/Grant Heilman ; A85(tr), William E. Ferguson; A85 (bl), Wilfred G. Iltis/William E. Ferguson; A85, (br), Michael J. Balick/Peter Arnold, Inc.; A86 (t), Arthur N. Orans/Murial Orans; A86 (b), E. R. Degginger/Color-Pic; A86 (cr), Jane Grushow/Grant Heilman ; A86(cl), Kevin Schafer/Peter Arnold, Inc.; A88, National Portrait Gallery; A8 (t), The Bettmann Archive; A90-A91 (bg), Wendell D. Metzen/Bruce Coleman, Inc.; A91 (l), David Young-Wolff/Photo Edit; A91(r), Lawrence Migdale/Stock, Boston; A92-A93 (bg), Grant Heilman/Grant Heilman ; A9 (b), Lee Foster/Bruce Coleman Inc. ; A94, Larry Lefever/Grant Heilman ; A95 (t), Runk Schoenberger/Grant Heilman .

Unit B: Harcourt Brace & Company Photographs: B4-B5, B6 (b), B7, B8, B9, B10-B11, B13, B15, B22, B24, B27 (l), B2 (r), B29, B39, B46, B49, B50(r), B55, B67(r), B74, B78, B82-B83, B85, B86(l), B90(t), B90(b), B94 (b).

All Other Photographs: Unit B Divider: Jeffrey L. Rotman/Peter Arnold, Inc. B1, Carl Roessler/Bruce Coleman, Inc.; B2-B3(bg), Carl Roessler/Bruce Coleman, Inc.; B3 (inset) Bob & Ira Spring; B6 (c), Greg Ryan-Sally Beyer; B12 (t), Tom Tracy/The Stock Market; B12 (bg), Uniphoto; B23 (l), Carl Purcell/Photo Researchers, Inc.; B23(r), Brian Parker/Tom Stack & Associates; B25, Johnny Johnson/Earth Scenes; B26, Kaz Mori/The Image Bank; B28, Four by Five; B30-B3 (bg), Jeff Dunn/Stock, Boston; B32, Larry Lefever/Grant Heilman ; B32-B33(bg), Clyde H. Smith/Peter Arnold, Inc.; B33 (l), Jim Strawser/Grant Heilman ; B33 (r), Thomas Hovland/Grant Heilman ; B36, Y.F. Chan/Superstock; B37, Jack Fields/Photo Researchers; B38 (c), Jeff Gnass/The Stock Market; B38(bg), David R. White/The Stock File; B38(inset) Lucy Ash/Rainbow; B40(l), W&D McIntyre/Photo Researchers; B40(r), NASA; B40(t), Erwin and Peggy Bauer/Bruce Coleman, Inc.; B41 (t), Kenneth W. Fink/Bruce Coleman, Inc.; B41(b), Schafer & Hill/Peter Arnold, Inc.; B42, G. Petrov/Washington Stock Photo; B43, G. Petrov/Washington Stock Photo; B44(l), E.R. Degginger/Bruce Coleman, Inc.; B44 (r), Kjell B. Sandved/Photo Researchers; B45(r), Michael Pitts/Animals, Animals, Inc.; B45(bg), Joy Spurr/Bruce Coleman, Inc.; B47, Jeffrey L. Rotman/Peter Arnold, Inc.; B48(t), Fred Bavendan/Peter Arnold, Inc.; B48(b), John Stern/Animals, Animals; B50(l), Michael P. Dadomski/Photo Researchers; B51

(t), Tom Bean/The Stock Market; B51(c), Patrick Grace/Photo Researchers; B51(b), Francious Gohier/Photo Researchers; B52(t), Carleton Ray/Photo Researchers; B52(c), Bill Wood/Bruce Coleman, Inc.; B52(b), Comstock; B53 (l), Scott Johnson/Animals Animals; B53(r), Allan Powe/Bruce Coleman, Inc.; B54(l), Patti Murray/Earth Scenes; B54(r), Scott Camazine/Photo Researchers; B56, Fred Bruemmer/Peter Arnold, Inc.; B58, Oxford Scientific Films/Animals Animals; B59(t), William E. Ferguson; B59 (b), Hans Reinhard/Bruce Coleman, Inc.; B60, (t), Australian Institute of Marine Science; B60, (b), Australian Institute of Marine Science; B62 (t), Ted Horowitz/The Stock Market; B62(inset) Jeff Gnass/The Stock Market; B64, George Herben/Alaska Stock Images; B65, Steve Arbrust/Alaska Stock Images; B66, Dan McCoy/Rainbow; B67 (l), McCoy/Rainbow; B68-B69, (spread) Randy Brandon/Alaska Stock Images; B70(t), Tom Bean; B70, (b), Gamma Liaison; B72, Earl Cryer/Gamma Liason; B73, Anchorage Daily News/Gamma Liason; B76 (t), Tom Myers; B76(b), Michael Baytoff/Black Star; B76-B77, Jeff Schultz/Alaska Stock Images; B77, (inset) Natalie B. Forbes; B79, Vanessa Vick/Photo Researchers; B80, Tom Myers; B81, Alissa Crandall/Alaska Stock Images; B86 (r), M.H. Colmenares; B88-B89(spread) John Scowen/FPG International; B89(l), Melissa Hayes English/Photo Researchers; B89(r), Brian Parker/Tom Stack & Associates; B91 (t), Al Grillo/Alaska Stock Images; B91 (b), David Young-Wolff/PhotoEdit; B92, Dan McCoy/Rainbow; B93, Scott Camazine/Photo Researchers; B94(t), John S. Flannery/Bruce Coleman, Inc.

Unit C: Harcourt Brace & Company Photographs: C3 (br), C4-C5, C7 (tr), C8, C9, C10-C11, C13, C14, C16, C19, C21, C29, C30, (t), C30(b), C31, C32 (b)C34, C35, C36, C37(t), C37(b), C38, C40, C41, C42, C43(r), C44(t), C44(b), C45 (t), C45 (c), C45(b), C46(r), C47, C50, C52, C53 (t), C53 (b), C57, C58, C59(t), C59(b), C60 (t), C68, C71 (r), C72(r), C77(r), C92 (t), C92(b), C93(b).

All Other Photographs: Unit C Divider: Mason Morfit/FPG; C1, FPG International; C2-C3(bg), FPG International; C6(t), FPG International; C6(c), The Bettmann Archive; C6(b), Al Assid/Stock Market, The; C7(c), Chuck O'Rear/Westlight; C7(b), Richard T. Nowitz; C7 (tl), The Granger Collection; C12(t), Mason Morfit/FPG International; C12(bg), Dan McCoy/Rainbow; C12, (inset) Gary Buss/FPG International; C18, David R. Frazier; C22-C23, (bg), Grant Faint/The Image Bank; C24, Paul Elsom/The Image Bank; C26(c), Smithsonian Institution; C26(b), The Granger Collection; C26(t), The Bettmann Archive; C27, The Bettmann Archive; C28-C29 (bg), Dan McCoy/Rainbow; C32(bg), Fukuhara/Westlight; C32(t), Chuck O'rear/Westlight; C33, W. Cody/Westlight; C34-C35(bg), Grant Faint/The Image Bank; C39(bg), Chuck O'Rear/Westlight; C46(bg), Comstock; C64(t), Bruce Forster/AllStock; C46, (inset), Michael Newman/PhotoEdit; C51, Richard Megna/Fundamental Photographs; C54(t), Susan Murray/Colorado Symphony; C54(b), Schlabowske/Time/Life Photo Lab; C55, Schlabowske/Time/Life Photo Lab; C60(b), Dr. Tony Brain/Science Photo Library/Photo Researchers; C62 (t), Stan Osolinski/Dembinsky Photo Association; C62(b), Franz Gorski/Animals-Animals; C63 (r), Peter Arnold, Inc.; C64 (l), The Granger Collection; C64 (r), The Granger Collection; C66-C67(bg), Larry Keenan Assoc./The Image Bank; C66(t), The Granger Collection; C66 (b), The Bettmann Archives; C67, The Image Works; C70 (l), Chuck O'Rear/Westlight; C70(r), Dan McCoy/Rainbow; C71(l), Frank Siteman/Photri Inc.; C72 (c), E. R. Degginger/Color-Pic; C76(t), The Bettmann Archives; C76(b), Stephen Simpson/FPG International; C80t), Tom Wilson/FPG International; C80(b), Robert E. Hager/FPG International; C80(cr), W.E.Roberts/Photoedit; C81(l), Eric Schnakenberg/FPG International; C83, Peter Menzel; C84, Peter Menzel; C85, Hank

Morgan/Rainbow; C87, Peter Menzel; C87, Peter Menzel; C88, Peter Menzel; C89, Peter Menzel;C90-C91, (bg), Alan Kearney/FPG; C91(l), Roy Morsch/Stock Market, The; C91 (r), Dan McCoy/Rainbow; C92-C93 (bg), Phillip M. Prosen/The Image Bank; C94(t), Montes De Oca/FPG International; C94(b), Fundamental Photographs; C95(l), E. R. Degginger/Color-Pic; C95 (r), Westlight; C96, Joe Baraban/The Stock Market.

Unit D: Harcourt Brace & Company Photographs: D4-D5, D6(t), D7(b), D8, D9, D10-D11, D19, D21, D24, D25(b), D31, D34, D43, D45 (all), D50, D53(l), D60, D61, D72, D73, D79, D82(l), D88, D92(t), D92(b), D93.

All Other Photographs: Unit D Divider: John Kieffer/Peter Arnold; D1, Tom Till; D2-D3(bg), Tom Till; D3(inset), Tom Till; D7(t), Gamma Liaison; D12(bg) Comstock; D12(t), Robert Falls/Bruce Coleman, Inc.; D12(b), E. R. Degginger/Color-Pic; D13t), Stephen Frisch/Stock, Boston; D13(b), Kevin Syms/David R. Frazier; D14(t), Tom Till; D14(b), William E. Ferguson; D15(l), E. R. Degginger/Color-Pic; D15(r), E. R. Degginger/Color-Pic; D18, Ferdinando Scianna/Magnum; D20(l), E. R. Degginger/Color-Pic; D20(r), E. R. Degginger/Color-Pic; D22(l), William E. Ferguson; D22(r), David R. Frazier; D23(tr), David. R. Frazier; D23 (bl), E. R. Degginger/Color-Pic; D23(bc), Art Resource; D23(br), E. R. Degginger/Color-Pic; D23(cr), E. R. Degginger/Color-Pic; D23 , Ron Kimball; D23, (tl), William E. Ferguson; D25(t), Eric A. Wessman/Stock, Boston; D26-D27(bg) Tom Till; D26(t), Tom Till; D26 (b), Tom Till; D27, Tom Till; D28 (t), Museum Of New Mexico; D28 (b), San Ildefonso polychrome, ca. 1922. Courtesy The Southwest Museum, Los Angeles ; D29 (t), Laboratory of Anthropology, Santa Fe.; D29(c), Laboratory of Anthropology, Santa Fe.; D29(b), Laboratory of Anthropology, Santa Fe.; D30 (bg) William E. Ferguson; D30 (t), John Kieffer/Peter Arnold, Inc.; D30(b), Tom Till; D32Ed Cooper Photography; D33t), Jim Steinberg/Photo Researchers; D33(b), The Image Works; D40, Nathen Benn/Stock, Boston; D40 (t), BPS/Terraphotographics; D41, (b)BPS/Terraphotographics; D42-D43(bg) Runk/Schoenberger/Grant Heilman; D44, BPS/Terraphotographics; D45b), Tom Till; D46(t), Tom Till; D46(c), Tom Till; D46(b), Joe Carrillo/Stock, Boston; D47 (t), Tom Till; D47(b), Tom Till; D48, Tom Till; D49(tr), Henry K. Kaiser/Leo de Wys Inc.; D49(bl), BPS/Terraphotographics; D49 (br), Dan Suzio/Photo Researchers; D49 (cl), Tom Till; D51 (l), Spencer Swanger/Tom Stack & Assoc.; D51 (r), Jack Fields/Photo Researchers; D51b), Ed Cooper Photography; D52(t), Greg Ryan & Sally Beyer; D52(b), Randall Hyman/Stock, Boston; D53 (r), David Wells/The Image Works; D54, Steve McCutcheon; D56(bg), William E. Ferguson; D56 (t), Bob Daemmrich/Stock, Boston; D56(inset) Tom Till; D58 (b), Peter Arnold/Peter Arnold, Inc.; D59 (t), Ken Lucas/BPS/Terraphotographics; D59(b), William E. Ferguson; D59 (c), J&L Weber/Peter Arnold, Inc.; D62 (t), William E. Ferguson; D62(b), Sinclair Stammers/Photo Researchers; D62, William E. Ferguson; D63 (t), B. Miller/BPS/Terraphotographics; D63(b), William E. Ferguson; D64(t), Francois Gohier/Photo Researchers; D64 (b), Tom McHugh/Nat. Museum of Nat. History; D65, William E. Ferguson; D66 (t), Saunders/BPS/Terraphotographics; D66(c), Itar-Tass/Sovoto; D66(b), Photo Researchers; D67(bg), William E. Ferguson; D70(l) William E. Ferguson; D70(r), William E. Ferguson; D71(l), Tom McHugh/National Museum of Natural History; D71((c), J&L Weber/Peter Arnold, Inc.; D71(r), PHoto Researchers; D76, (bg), Art Wolfe/AllStock; D76 (t), Stephen Frink/Waterhouse Stock Photo; D76(t), Terry Donnelly/Dembinsky Photo Assoc.; D76 (b), Gordon Wiltsie/Peter Arnold, Inc.; D77(b), Crandall/The Image Works; D78-D79 (bg), Art Wolfe/AllStock; D80(l), Tom Myers; D80 (r), Bill

Gallery/Stock, Boston; D81 (t), Billy Barnes; D81(b), Cary Wolinsky/Stock, Boston; D82(r), Martin Miller/Positive Image; D84(l), Ed Cooper Photography; D84 (r), Joseph Solem/Camera Hawaii; D85(t), J. Robert Stottlemyer/Biological Photo Service; D85 (c), W.L. McCoy/McCoy's Image Studio; D85(b), Bob & Ira Spring; D86(t), Julie Houck/Stock, Boston; D86(c), Jeff Foott/Tom Stack & Assoc.; D86(b), David Young-Wolf/PhotoEdit; D87, (l), Laurance B. Aiuppy; D87(r), Laurance B.Aiuppy; D90-D91(bg), Ruch Buzzelli/Tom Stack & Assoc.; D91 (l), Ken Lucas/Biological Photo Service; D91(r), Dembinski Photo Assoc.; D94, (inset) Breck P. Kent/Earth Scenes; D94, Franco Salmoiraghi/The Stock Market; D95, Art Wolfe/AllStock.

Unit E: Harcourt Brace & Company Photographs: E7, E8, E9, E10-E11, E14, E22, E23, E25, E26, E36, E39, E40, E44, E53, E57(tl), E61, E62, E65(b), E76 (t).

All Other Photographs: Unit E Divider: H. Mark Weidman; E1, Tom Till; E2-E3(bg), Tom Till; E3, (inset) Thomas R. Fletcher/Stock, Boston; E6, Murial Orans; E12(t), J. Lotter/Tom Stack & Assoc.; E12(inset) E. R. Degginger/Color-Pic; E12(border) FPG Internatinal; E13, H. Mark Weidman; E15(r), Coco McCoy/Rainbow; E15(r), Ira Spring; E18(t), Tom Stack & Assoc.; E18(b), John Gerlach/Tom Stack & Assoc.; E21 (t), H. Mark Weidman; E21 (c), William E. Ferguson; E21(b), Murial Orans; E21(bg), Brain Parker/Tom Stacks & Assoc.; E30, H. Mark Weidman; E38, (bg), Superstock; E38, (t), Ed Cooper PhotoraphE; E38, (inset) William E. Ferguson; E41 (l), Mark C. Burnett; E41 (r), Mark C. Burnett; E41 (b), Mark C. Burnett; E42, Charlie Ott Photography/Photo Reseachers; E43(c), William E. Ferguson Photography; E43(b), BPS/Terraphotographics; E47 (t), Rod Plank/Dembinsky Photo Association; E48, Stephen E. Cornelius/Photo Researchers; E50(bg), Uniphoto; E50(t), Uniphoto; E50, (inset) Aaron Haupt/David R. Frazier; E51, (t), Erich Geduldig/Naturbild/OKAPIA/Photo Researchers, Inc.; E51(b), David E. Frazier; E54 (c), E. R. Degginger/Color-Pic; E54(tl), E. R. Degginger/Color-Pic; E54(tr), Jerome Wexler/Photo Researchers; E54(bl), Phil Degginger/Color-Pic; E54(br), E. R. Degginger/Color-Pic; E55 (tl), Hermann Eisenbeiss/Photo Researchers; E55(tr), Michael P. Gadomski/Photo Researchers; E55 (bl), Murial Orans; E55(br), William E. Ferguson; E56(tl), Alvin E. Staffan/Photo Researchers; E56 (tr), E. R. Degginger/Color-Pic; E56 (bl), Aaron Haupt/David E. Frazier; E56 (br), M.L.Dembinsky, Jr. / Dembinsky Photo Assoc.; E56(cl), Kenneth Murray/Photo Researchers; E56(cr), William E. Ferguson; E57(tr), E. R. Degginger/Color-Pic; E57(bl), Gary Retherford/Photo Researchers; E57(br), Kjell B. Sandved/Photo Researchers; E59(l), Dale Nichols/Rich Franco Photography; E59(r), Terry Donnelly/Dembinsky Photo Assos.; E64-E65(t), G.V. Faint/The Image Bank; E66 (t), E. R. Degginger/Color-Pic; E66(b), Harry Rogers/Photo Researchers; E67(t), Bonnie Rauch/Photo Researchers; E67(c), David R. Frazier; E67(b), Leonide Principe/Photo Researchers; E68(t), E. R. Degginger/Color-Pic; E68 (c), E. R. Degginger/Color-Pic; E68 (b), Camera Hawaii; E69 (t), William E.Ferguson; E69 (c), Dwight Kuhn; E69(b), E. R. Degginger/Color-Pic; E70, Walter Chandoha,; E71(c), Ian J. Adams/ Dembinsky Photo Assoc.; E71 (c), William E. Ferguson; E71(tr), Willard Clay/Dembinsky Photo Assoc.; E71 (bl), Ken Brate/Photo Researchers Inc.,E71 (br), Scott Camazine/Photo Researchers Inc.,E72 (t), Ronald Nagata, Sr.; E72-E73(b), Ronald Nagata, Sr.; E74(inset) David R. Frazier; E74-75(bg), William M. Partington/Photo Researchers Inc.; E75(inset) Gary Braasch/Woodfin Camp & Assoc.; E76 (t),Tony Freeman/PhotoEdit; E77(t), Larry Lefever/Grant Heilman ; E77 (b), Hank Morgan/Photo Researchers Inc.; E78(l), Runk Schoenberger/Grant Heilman .